AN EPICUREAN ODYSSEY

A ROAD TRIP AROUND NEW ZEALAND

BY ROBERT GIORGIONE

Books by the same author:

"An Epicurean Odyssey: Sommelier Stories"
"The Roving Sommelier's Bucket List of New Zealand Wines"

An Epicurean Odyssey: A Road Trip Around New Zealand is a personalised journey through food and wine, embellished with many mouth-watering anecdotes, recipes and wine pairings.

ISBN 978-1-291-52169-6 Revised Edition. Spring 2015

Cover photograph: "Nin's Bin" Crayfish Shack, Kaikoura Coast, South Island, New Zealand. © Copyright Robert Giorgione 2009

CONTENTS

"Wine is one of the most civilised and most natural things in the world that has been brought to the greatest perfection and it offers a greater range of enjoyment and appreciation than possibly any other purely sensory thing"
Ernest Hemingway

AN EPICUREAN ODYSSEY

"An Epicurean Odyssey: A Road Trip Around New Zealand" is my first book and the first in a series of vinous road trips. Essentially, it is a personalised journey through food and wine, embellished with many mouth-watering anecdotes, recipes and wine pairings. Each book within this series will follow a general theme and will provide an insight into the country, its people, cultural diversity and regional produce. I have matched more than 80 recipes from family, friends and colleagues with my own personal wine suggestions. The book also features useful maps, references, local specialities, places of interest to visit, including vineyards, restaurants, bars and farmers markets, places to stay and links to many websites, blog articles, photos and videos.

My aim is to provide you with a snapshot of the country through evocative memories and experiences. This is the revised edition of my original book which I wrote and self-published between 2009 and 2011 and contains a host of fresh and updated content.

I would like to pay tribute to all my family and friends in New Zealand, especially Fred, Nancy, Ray and Lee. In addition, many thanks to all the wonderful people I have met and who supported me along the way, especially Sandy and Nicki for their friendship and good times.

Arohanui!

Robert Giorgione Spring 2015

A portion of my book sales will be donated to the New Zealand Earthquake Appeal Fund.

FOREWORD

"We admire and strive for perfection, for that 'greatness'. You can hear it in the conversations; there is a restlessness, a constant looking forward. Our family table has only twelve seats, saved for twelve wine making families from around our country. We each bring to the table only what is good enough to be shared by the family seated, so if it's not in the glass at our table, it certainly won't be going to yours."

William Hoare (Fromm Winery, Marlborough) - Chairman The Family of Twelve

To watch this video , please scan QR code with your smartphone.

David Cox - Former Director New Zealand Wine Growers (Europe)

INTRODUCTION

When it comes to New Zealand, I have many memories and to be honest the majority of them are very positive. The first things which spring to mind are family, friends and rugby. For me, wine and food came later. When I was much younger, we were told stories about our relatives (mainly on my mother's side), who came from the Southern Hemisphere. In fact, both my maternal grandparents came from big families and some decided many years ago to settle elsewhere in very remote and far flung places such as Australia and New Zealand. At a tender age, listening to all these anecdotes was very interesting, perhaps exotic, even though it is generally typical for most British families to have relations out there. I distinctly remember looking at the photos of various aunts, uncles and cousins and hoping one day to meet them and to be able to visit such a beautiful country.

I was named after my grandfather, Robert (a.k.a Bob Hill) who sadly passed away at the ripe age of 94 towards the end of 2012 and was patriarch of the family. His two younger siblings, Fred and Ray, (my great uncles) went to New Zealand many years ago and settled just outside Wellington. Fred, the elder of the two brothers, married Nancy and had a daughter Lucy (who currently resides in Auckland). They first lived in a suburb of the city and then moved to Waikanae on the picturesque Kapiti Coast. Ray, the youngest member of the Hill clan got married to Lee, decided to live and work in Upper Hutt, just north of Wellington and had three children of their own: Francesca, Robert and Trevor. So, in a nutshell, those are my family links to the country. Great uncle Fred has also passed away and Ray, now in his mid-seventies, still plays squash regularly at his local club and continues to enjoy life. In addition, my great-grandmother (originally from Devon, South-West England) was buried in Wellington. These stories about New Zealand initially came from my grandparents, who travelled there in the late 1970s and early 1980s. For me, one stand out memory completely encapsulated the sheer remoteness and sparseness of the country when my grandfather mentioned the distinct lack of traffic on the roads and how Uncle Fred said: "This is our Waikanae rush-hour traffic jam" – waiting a mere few minutes for three cars to pass. You will begin to realise that traffic (or the lack of it, especially in some parts) is a common theme, which crops up from time to time throughout this book.

Secondly, the New Zealand wine industry was still very basic and in its infancy. The trend was to produce sweetish and Germanic styles of wines, from grapes such as Muller-Thurgau and so on. I recall my grandfather telling me the delights of a local wine in Marlborough called a "Blenheimer", which was rather like a cross between a regular fruity white wine and Sauternes. There were tales of "booze barns" and huge supermarkets called "Pack'n'Save". I remember the decorative Maori carvings, distinctive jade and beautiful paua shells my Nonna brought back with her. The food, on the other hand, from what I gather was even simpler. Apparently, the Kiwis are rather fond of their pies and homely comfort food. Overall, I got the impression that New Zealand was rather like England back in the 1950s. For some reason I was completely fascinated. Some people seem to share an affinity or bond with a country or culture and for me it has always been New Zealand. I do not really know how to explain it, but from that moment on, I said to myself that one day, given the opportunity, I would love to visit that country. Who knows, perhaps even one day I may live there myself. The language barrier would not pose too much of a problem either.

Speaking of language and culture, we are literally talking a different 'lingo' here too. My first experience of this was back in 1980 when we lived in Oxford and I met a Kiwi boy at school called David James. We went to school together in Summertown. In fact, I used to walk past Raymond Blanc's first place "Le Petit Blanc" in that little arcade each day en route. Perhaps this was a sign of greater things to come, which would also inspire me with my gastronomic education and journey? At that time I was certainly not inspired by New Zealand for its food. I used to laugh when my friend David, who came from Rotorua, brought cold toast to school. Yes, you heard me correctly, cold toast. During our morning break, we would either go to the tuck shop and purchase some sweets or munch on our own snacks which we had brought from home. David brought his cold toast. Was this some kind of new food trend, of which I was not aware? I distinctly remember that not only was this rather quirky and completely alien to me, even though I do rather like toast, but he put things like cinnamon on it. He also spoke English with a funny accent and ended pretty much each sentence with "eh?". The pair of us hit it off and we became best mates, even with our own rudimentary sense of taste. We soon gave the situation a competitive twist to see who could make the most creative cold toast sandwich. Of course, the fragrant cinnamon was regarded 'extremely sophisticated', but the lemon curd got my vote. At the time, my mum probably thought this weird and seeing as I was around nine or ten years old, wine was still off the agenda. I was starting my culinary adventure and with my new Kiwi friend, we began to stimulate our innocent taste buds. Not exactly 'epicurean' you may remark, yet we all had to start somewhere. We appreciate that tastes and smells can be very evocative. I have a kind of 'David James cold toast moment' whenever I smell cinnamon. By the way, I do like Marmite and share my late Nonna's love of Vegemite, which of course is rather different.

I played squash and a bit of rugby at school and still really enjoy both games. In fact, I adore watching sports too. As with most people, I would regard the New Zealand "All Blacks" as the best team in the World. Regardless of the fact whether they are currently Number 1 or 3 or whatever in the World, they are always considered by rugby fans the team to beat. Over the years I have been to quite a few matches and if you ever get the opportunity to watch them, especially when they perform "The Haka", it is always such a thrilling spectacle. You feel the hairs on the back of your neck and a little emotional lump in your throat too. Essentially, this energy, intensity, pride and spirituality probably sum my feelings towards New Zealand. It was back in 1987, the inaugural year of the "Rugby World Cup" that I actually sipped on a New Zealand wine for the first time. I think it was something straight forward and generic and most definitely a Sauvignon Blanc from a vineyard such as Corbans or Nobilo. During 1988, while working in restaurants and before departing to university, I tasted more wines and decided to set up my wine collection. Let us just say the rest is history and how things have changed dramatically.

When I came to London in 1996, I decided to specialise in wine and focused my career on becoming a sommelier. I have been a sommelier ever since and my work ethic is still that of one. As you can imagine, even though I am now self employed and have my own business, I have tasted many wines from all around the World. For instance back then, whilst I was sommelier at Oxo Tower Restaurant, the first Kiwi wines I listed and became familiar with were from Kumeu River, Isabel Estate, Cloudy Bay, Seresin, Kim Crawford, Te Mata, Ata Rangi, Palliser Estate, Martinborough Vineyards and Neudorf, amongst others. I had the opportunity and good fortune to meet many influential people within the wine business for whom I have great admiration and have inspired me during the course of my journey. In addition, I have very fond memories of the diners drinking crisp and fruity Kiwi Sauvignon Blanc in the places where I have worked as if they couldn't get enough of it. Many years later, allegedly, we are all still on the crest of that wave.

Owing to my love of New Zealand, I also decided to 'specialise' to a certain degree with the country's wines. Over the years, through tasting the wines and meeting the wine makers, not only have I continued to learn more about them, but also about the places and people behind them; it has been a stimulating education. I have been fortunate enough to work with and for some amazing people and can count many of these as genuine friends. Most satisfyingly, I have managed to turn my hobby into my career and every day I go to work, I am discovering something new. Under the guise of 'roving sommelier' I enthusiastically enjoy communicating and sharing my experiences and am trying to inspire you with confidence to discover your own taste. Food, wine and travel can bring all of us together.

The first time I visited New Zealand was 2001. My best friend and soul-mate Sandy, whom I met in London in 2000, had emigrated to Auckland and I travelled with my sister to visit her and the rest of my family. It was also during the same year that Peter Gordon and Michael McGrath opened up The Providores Restaurant and Tapa Room in Marylebone. I admire Peter and Michael, not only as restaurateurs, but also as people. I have been a big fan of Peter's cooking ever since the heydays of The Sugar Club in Notting Hill during the 1990s. We have become good friends and I always enjoy going to their restaurants. Rest assured this dynamic Kiwi duo, amongst many others who I have encountered along the way will be featured throughout this book. Things have also come around full circle, as they opened up a brand new version of The Sugar Club in Auckland in 2013.

Since 2002, I have travelled extensively around New Zealand many times and spent valuable time with wonderful individuals and businesses. This enabled me to gain a much better understanding of and further insight into the country and its people. I even gained some memorable hands-on experience during a couple of vintage harvests. By reading my blog articles and wine reviews, scanning the QR codes, watching and engaging in my roving sommelier videos and clicking on the links to hundreds of websites contained within this book, I sincerely hope that you will enjoy and be able to relate to these experiences too.

My main aim with this 'road trip' style book and via the anecdotes and rich content within is to demonstrate that New Zealand has indeed its very own wine and food identity based upon a heritage rooted in family tradition, an energetic spirit, a cultural melting pot and an innovative blend of tastes and flavours, which express their own sense of place. So sit back and relax and let me be your friendly tour guide on the epicurean odyssey. Please ensure you bring a healthy appetite and I hope you enjoy our journey.

Robert Giorgione (a.k.a The Roving Sommelier)

"If it would not look too much like showing off, I would tell the reader where New Zealand is."
Mark Twain

NEW ZEALAND

AN OVERVIEW OF NEW ZEALAND WINE

Before we get started together on this journey around New Zealand, let us embrace a few words from arguably the country's finest chef, Peter Gordon.

"In 1981 I started a Horticultural Science Degree at Massey University in Palmerston North, in order to become a wine maker. An actual degree specifically for this career didn't exist then. Cloudy Bay wines hadn't quite set the world alight at this point in history, and to be honest I'd only drunk cask wine or sweet Muller Thurgau wines myself and had no idea what the world of wine had to offer. I only lasted one term before setting sail for Australia, and embarking on my true love, cooking, but I often wonder where I might be now had I stuck to the grape and not the pan. These days New Zealand is world renowned for its wines – from the Marlborough Sauvignon Blancs from those years past, through to gorgeous silky Pinot Noir from Otago, Martinborough and Marlborough. Hawke's Bay produces amazing Bordeaux blends and Chardonnay. Pinot Gris and Viognier are as likely to be planted as Riesling, Tempranillo, Gewürztraminer or any one of many varietals. Our wine industry is huge compared to what it once was, although compared to the output of Bordeaux, we're quite tiny – but most New Zealanders are now up to speed with what they prefer to drink with dinner and why they like a particular varietal. Our wines are increasingly found around the globe and as I type this a Chinese TV crew are here at my restaurant in Auckland, dine by Peter Gordon, and they're filming my food alongside several Marlborough wines, which is where they're headed tomorrow. Suddenly our audience, and the potential consumer base, will increase by an estimated 250 million. So I think we can safely predict the future of the industry is bright – and once you try a top quality NZ wine, it's hard to ignore."

Peter Gordon – co-owner and executive chef of The Providores Restaurant, Bar and Tapa Room, Marylebone, London.

New Zealand has traditionally been an agricultural country, with its exports dominated by meat and dairy products, but the last three decades have seen a greater diversity of new produce from fruit, vegetables and nuts to wine and olive oil. At the same time, there has been a proliferation of top-notch restaurants and cafes, and a growing range of new foods available. Primarily, the cosmopolitan cities and centres of tourism such as Auckland, Wellington and Queenstown are leading the way. But if you stray off the beaten track you will surely encounter some excellent places to visit, eat, drink and stay and enjoy the friendly hospitality for which the Kiwis are known.

In my opinion, the watershed year for New Zealand was 1999. Two important events happened, which had a dramatic effect on their tourism as a result. Auckland hosted the Americas Cup Yacht Race, and the epic "Lord of the Rings" film was launched onto the world stage. Ever since that time, New Zealand has become a major destination for the global traveller. However, in typical imitable Kiwi style, they did not just sit back and wait for the curious masses to come and visit them. They energetically pushed forwards and really went for tourism in a big way. Generally Kiwis do not rest on their laurels and they are always trying to improve. It is probably that competitive spirit mixed with the right amount of down-to-earth humility which makes them a great nation. Moreover, with this abundance of delicious, fresh produce and influences from elsewhere, the talented chefs and purveyors have a whole array of fish, seafood, lamb, beef, venison, fruits and vegetables at their disposal.

New Zealand is unique. Almost hidden away in a remote corner of the globe is a place of glorious unspoiled landscapes, exotic flora and fauna and a culture renowned for its spirit of youthful innovation. New Zealand is a world of pure discovery and nothing distils its essence more perfectly than a glass of New Zealand wine. Basically, the country of New Zealand is comprised of two large and long islands, which have been named (very easy for travellers to remember) North Island and South Island. An isolated South Pacific island nation with a temperate climate, New Zealand or Aotearoa ("Land of the Long White

Cloud") enjoys undeniable advantages when it comes to producing ultra premium wines. The proximity of the vineyards to the ocean has a pronounced effect on the personality and character of the wines. However, there are very big differences between the "Top of the North" and the "Bottom of the South". Without doubt though, one thing you will experience when you go there is the stunning landscape.

Good food calls for good wine and with all of these ingredients, my aim is to express a genuine regionality of the country via its food and wine pairings. New Zealand's wine industry is surging ahead, with the number of wineries increasing dramatically, and the wines winning medals and admirers globally. It is safe to say that never have Kiwi wines been more popular. Mild, sunny summers and marked differences between day- and night-time temperatures (a.k.a diurnal range) in many regions slow the ripening of the grapes and allow them to develop intense and varietal flavours. These characteristics are the very core of the country's wines' elegance and purity, and explain their famed harmony, structure and food-friendliness. The topography of the land also has a key influence on the wines' personality. For instance, the regional diversity is dramatic, enabling a striking array of wine styles to flourish. It is very easy to generalise, but not all Kiwi wines taste the same.

New Zealand's history of wine production goes back to the 1800s. But the real catalyst was during the 1980s when the astonishingly different Marlborough Sauvignon Blanc was unleashed onto the international wine scene. It was certainly the first Kiwi wine I ever tasted and perhaps it was for you too. While Marlborough retains its status as one of the world's foremost wine producing regions, the quality of wines from elsewhere in the country has also garnered international acclaim. For instance, the great Pinot Noirs from the established vineyards of Nelson, Martinborough and Waipara and from the exciting and up-and-coming region of Central Otago in the South. Bordeaux blend reds (Cabernets and Merlot) and peppery Syrah are well-suited to the soils and micro-climates of Waiheke Island, Martinborough and the Gimblett Gravels in Hawke's Bay. This is the very tip of the iceberg and throughout this book I will show you a lot more. Even with one grape variety such as Sauvignon Blanc, you will begin to realise the various regional differences and sub-regional nuances in tastes and flavours ranging from saline, mineral, asparagus, gooseberry, herbaceous and nettle through to pungent and aromatic capsicum, tropical, passion fruit and stone fruit. My aim is to help you discover the true pleasure of wine and for you to hopefully go on and enjoy many more moments. After all, I know what I like, but it does not necessarily mean that you will like it too. Taste is very personal. To begin with it is best to keep an open mind. We will also have some fun along the way - it's so simple. And though the current average price tag for a New Zealand wine is a reflection of its desirability, few would question its ability to deliver excellent value for money. It is hard to think of a more satisfying opportunity for self-improvement than tasting wines with or without food. Please enjoy the adventure in making a discovery. For me, it is a genuine pleasure to share this with you. But let's keep it real. So, before we get into the nitty-gritty of regions and grape varieties, here are a few more choice words from David Cox describing the success of the Kiwi savvy - Sauvignon Blanc: perhaps New Zealand's greatest success story.

"Quite simply, the cool-climate style that New Zealand has produced from this grape variety, especially in Marlborough, has completely captivated the consumer. It commands a premium price, yet consumers love it and there is no evidence that this will change. Some say this success means that Sauvignon Blanc is the only grape variety that people think of when considering wines from New Zealand, and there is no doubt that one of the priorities of the generic body of New Zealand Winegrowers is to broaden awareness of the country's other varieties such as Pinot Noir, Syrah, Chardonnay, Pinot Gris, Riesling and Bordeaux Blends. Let's not forget that Marlborough was sheep-grazing land just 30 years ago. Kiwi Sauvignon Blanc will remain our signature grape: it is alive and kicking and has a long, prosperous life ahead of it."

Let us go all the way back to 1982. Remember I was telling you about my grandparents? Well, fortunately and probably like most of us, when we go travelling we usually bring back souvenirs and brochures. I always manage to acquire a suitcase full of various bits and bobs, including gifts and mementos. Like many other grandparents, mine had bookshelves stacked full of books, pamphlets and maps of all the places they had visited on their jaunts. Some of these were passed on to me, especially as we shared our passion for foreign travel. Recently, I flicked through a New Zealand guide from 1982, written by T.B McDonald and Terry Dunleavy, both of the NZ Wine Institute based in Auckland. I was amazed to discover that back then the wines were mainly made from Chasselas, Muller-Thurgau and quirky other hybrids. The basic wine nomenclature also included such terminology as "Rhine Riesling" and "Chablis". Of course, things have been smartened up considerably since.

"The next few years will be even more exciting and new grape varieties will be introduced which look like being even more suited to our environment, and we quicken the pace of developing a truly unique New Zealand wine style, for sale on an international wine market which is constantly seeking wines which are different. Wine making is essentially a personal art, and the principal objective is to bring enjoyment and satisfaction to people. Our industry adds something of value to our New Zealand way of life. Wine is best enjoyed in moderation, and in company, especially of kindred souls," says Terry Dunleavy.

Key dates in the early New Zealand wine timeline

1819: Samuel Marsden planted first European vines at Kerikeri.
1833: James Busby planted vineyard at Waitangi – the first known to produce wine.
1850s: Mission Estate, New Zealand's oldest winery established in Taradale, near Napier in Hawke's Bay.
1880: Anthony Vidal established vineyard in Hawke's Bay (currently owned by Villa Maria).
1895: Romeo Bragato, Italian viticulturist, was invited by the Government to tour the country to investigate the potential for a local wine industry.

1902: Yugoslavian immigrants established Pleasant Valley vineyard in Henderson.

1934: Ivan Yukich planted vines in West Auckland and established Montana.

During the 1960s and '70s: Innovation and extensive plantings of Germanic varietals. Relaxation of wine laws leading up to 1976 when caterers and wineries were allowed to serve alcohol and in 1979 when the first wine bar licence was granted.

1973: First vineyards established in the Wairau River Valley in Marlborough by Montana (now known as Brancott Estate).

Mid-late 1970s: Seifried and Finn families settled in Nelson and planted vines at Appleby and Moutere.

Late 1970s and early '80s: First plantings of Pinot Noir in Martinborough.

Mid-1970s and early '80s: Real progress made in Hawke's Bay by pioneers such as John Buck at Te Mata and John Hancock at Trinity Hill. First Syrah vines planted by Allan Limmer at Stonecroft. First vines planted by Goldwater family on Waiheke Island.

Early 1980s: Early trailblazers in Marlborough such as Allan Scott, Jane Hunter, the Spence Brothers and Montana, amongst others proving successful with Sauvignon Blanc.

1985: First vintage for Cloudy Bay in Marlborough.

1986: First vineyard established in Central Otago by Allan Brady at Gibbston Valley.

1980s: Pioneer wine maker Daniel Schuster gaining success in Canterbury and Michael Brajkovich (New Zealand's first MW) created a new style of Chardonnay at Kumeu River, that went on to be considered the country's benchmark.

These guys obviously had a clear vision of what the land could naturally produce, yet could still fulfil and deliver their aspirations. Together with other pioneers and founders of the New Zealand wine industry they helped everyone and generations that have followed in their footsteps to get where they are now.

There's something about the fermented grape juice business that keeps it in families, in many cases for centuries. While elsewhere "family" and "business" are increasingly separate concepts, in wine they remain, more often than not, proudly united. The handful of Dalmatian families which settled around Auckland, originally to work on the farms and forests, brought over with them to New Zealand their own wine culture and heritage. They formed the bedrock of the New Zealand wine business. Wine starts with the land. Many of the wine regions are still relatively young, but as second and third generations join the pioneers, the secrets of the land are being unlocked and passed on, creating fine wines and wine makers in the process. The best wines are based on an intense interrogation of the land, a mature appreciation of the possibilities and limits. A measure of this maturity is the fact we no longer simply talk about the land, but about the much wider concept of 'terroir'. Wine has now become as much a part of New Zealand's national being as whitebait, meat pies, rugby and pavlova.

Here's a few choice words from a couple of eminent Kiwi wine experts:

"Most people, if they have a view of New Zealand - have a positive one: mainly physical beauty and maybe wine. Maybe the Brits have a broader view: they tend to like Kiwis, partly because we are not Australian. We are seen to share a positive and easy-going character with the Aussies. I think my upbringing informs my approach to wine. I have no time for pretension or snobbery in wine; I want people to discover the joys of wine and learn to trust their own judgment. If I can help them, that's great"
Peter McCombie MW - wine communicator

"The most exciting things in New Zealand Wine currently are the refinements and developments taking place with Chardonnay; the impact in quality that vine age clearly brings to Pinot Noir and how regional characteristics are beginning to show in our noble varieties like Sauvignon Blanc, Pinot and Syrah. I am most excited about the future of Syrah, Riesling and Methode Traditionnelle expressions." Cameron Douglas MS - wine communicator

Speaking in a wine sense, even though its heritage goes as far back as the mid-1800s, New Zealand as a wine-producing country is very much "New World" as opposed to the "Old World" of its European counterparts. Hence, you should find the wine's main grape variety on the label. You will also find the name of the vineyard and region. It is important to remember, however, that in a very modern sense, the New Zealand wine industry only really took off since the early 1980s. In 1973, Montana (now known as Brancott Estate) were the first to plant a vineyard in Marlborough and it was during the late 1970s and early 1980s that the first Kiwi Sauvignon Blancs were produced and sold commercially. 1985 saw the first vintage of a wine produced under the now-iconic Cloudy Bay label. During the late 1970s and early 80s, the first Pinot Noir vines were being planted within Martinborough, Waipara and Nelson. The thing about wine is – just as each bottle is in a constant state of metamorphosis, so too is the industry. It is all very exciting now - boundaries are being pushed, new benchmarks are being set, our appetite for quality, innovation and new wine styles is as strong as ever and look at how quickly things have developed, not only within New Zealand itself, but also internationally. But let us not forget those original few individuals, pioneers, trailblazers and heroes who helped to shape and influence the way their nation's wines were made and continue to be produced and perceived. Surely they deserve huge recognition for their hard work and devotion to their craft and we can certainly learn something positive from their experience? After all, they seem very happy to share their wisdom and pass on their savoir faire to the next generation.

Please note: all vineyards mentioned are personal recommendations and include wines that I believe are good representations of their region and wine style. There are plenty more wineries and vineyards featured within each regional chapter. I have some great content, including many wine reviews, food and wine matching ideas and roving sommelier videos with legendary wine makers and viticulturists in the web links index at the back of this book.

Sauvignon Blanc

It is now considered that, on a par with the Loire Valley in France, New Zealand sets the benchmark for this grape variety. However, as a general rule of thumb, the Kiwi version is less subtle and more pungently aromatic and explosively flavoured in style. Regional nuances can range from tropical flavours in the warmer climates of Auckland, Gisborne and Hawke's Bay to fresh and clean gooseberry and asparagus of the Wairarapa. Within the South Island, and Marlborough itself, where the majority of this grape is grown, you now have a diverse range of flavours, including those 'classic' characteristics of zesty and vibrant fruit intensity of the Wairau River Valley to the more nettle and capsicum of the Southern and Awatere Valleys. Nelson produces excellent fruity savvies and further South in Central Otago they display much more minerality and a crisper acidity on the finish.

In a relatively short space of time, Sauvignon Blanc has become New Zealand's internationally-recognised flagship varietal. In fact it makes up more than three-quarters of the country's grape production, with the majority of that planted in Marlborough. The first vineyard to be planted with Sauvignon was in 1973 when Montana took cuttings of this new grape from vines grown in the Auckland region. Montana has subsequently changed its name to Brancott Estate, which is also the location of the annual Marlborough Wine Festival held each February. Enthusiasm for Sauvignon Blanc continues and, although Marlborough growers have successfully introduced other varietals, Sauvignon is still the region's most popular wine style.

For me, New Zealand Sauvignon Blanc can be split into two disinctive styles - 'Classic' and 'Reserve and/or oak-aged'. Within both categories I believe there is a breadth of choice. Of course, it's all a question of taste and you will decide which you prefer. However, you will have to agree that currently and especially within Marlborough the wine making boundaries are being pushed like never before. Just take a good look at what the likes of Ivan Sutherland, James Healy, Kevin Judd, Tamra Washington and Brian Bicknell, amongst others are doing.

The majority of New Zealand Sauvignon Blanc is cold fermented in temperature controlled stainless steel tanks. This style has become what is regarded as the 'classic' New Zealand Sauvignon Blanc - crisp, dry, fruit-driven, explosively-aromatic with delicious mouth-watering acidity. Such is our appetite for this wine that it is normally released very quickly and the bottles are on the shelves in our supermarkets in around six months after harvest. Even though most people choose to enjoy this wine when it's very young and at its vibrant best, don't be fooled by older vintages of Sauvignon, as some of them, in the right vintage, have the ability to age quite well.

An emerging and exciting wine style that is starting to become very popular is the oaked-aged Sauvignon Blanc. As mentioned earlier, most vineyards produce the 'classic' style of Sauvignon Blanc, yet some vintners are also experimenting with the use of oak and other winemaking tricks to add complexity into their wines. The first to produce this completely different style of Sauvignon was Cloudy Bay with their iconic "Te Koko". It went on to be a commercial smash and blazed a different kind of Sauvignon trail for others to follow. Other vineyards took their lead and have gone on to successfully produce oaked or reserve styles. For me, they are very expressive, extremely food-friendly and generally very interesting. Not only are these oak-aged wines more complex and flavoursome, but also they have many layers of texture on the palate. It also shows that the nation's wine makers and viticultrists are attempting to push the boundaries with their wines, trying to make them more interesting and different. They also appeal to a more sophisticated palate.

Whilst on my 2014 trip around New Zealand, I visited Giesen vineyard and was very pleased to see what they are currently doing. Alongside their 'regular' wines, which are very well-made, typical examples of Marlborough savvy, they are also producing a range of single vineyard wines that have been aged in old 1000 litre German 'Fuder' barrels. I tasted all of them and I have to admit they were good. For me, it shows that Giesen have upped their game and are trying to make an inter-esting and very expressive range of wines, yet haven't compromised on their family tradition and quality.

Notable Marlborough examples include: Ara, Astrolabe, Auntsfield, Brancott Estate, Clos Henri, Cloudy Bay, Dog Point, Giesen, Greywacke, Hunter's, Invivo, Isabel Estate, Jackson Estate, Mahi, Nautilus, Palliser Estate, Saint Clair, Seresin Estate, Tarras, Terravin, Vavasour, Villa Maria, Woollaston and Yealands Estate, amongst many others.

Riesling

I have a saying: "When you say Riesling, you smile…" Not only is it true, but also I adore this grape variety with a passion. In January 2011 I presented 75 Rieslings from around the world, including 22 from New Zealand at my "Ravenous For Riesling" blind tasting. There is a link containing the full article and line up of wines at the back of this book. With Riesling, New Zealand has started to display some real expression and diversity. I love its clean-as-a-whistle, zesty, citrus fruit character, ranging from lemon and lime to pink grapefruit, interspersed with red apple and stone fruit nuances, yet always with that signature mouth-watering acidity and freshness. It can also display an almost-Germanic floral quality and personality, normally being lower in alcohol which is pleasantly appealing. For me, it is the most food-friendly of grape varieties. Rest assured there will be plenty of super-fresh Riesling recom-mendations here. Great micro-climates proving suitable for Riesling are: Martinborough, Marlborough, Nelson, Waipara and Central Otago.

Dry, aromatic wines are extremely good matches for spicy dishes and seafood. Alternatively, owing to their relatively low alcohol, New Zealand Rieslings are very refreshing and just lovely to sip on a warm summer's day. In addition, if you ever wish to experience aromatic wines to the fullest, then head to Nelson and enjoy their beautiful wines, picturesque scenery and wonderful local arts and crafts scene during the annual Nelson Wine Art Festival. Tim and Judy Finn of Neudorf Vineyards, Craig Potton and various art galleries, restaurants and artisan craft breweries collaborate together and put on a great show of local produce. It's a real must-visit.

"It should come as no surprise that New Zealand Riesling grows so well in the most beautiful parts of the country- Central Otago, North Canterbury, Marlborough & Nelson. Here you'll find searing mountain tops of acidity, beautiful only because of the contrast of the sweet, lush valleys in-between. There are twisting, turning threads of roads, balanced knife edge like on blustery ridges. The heady mix of aromatics created by a land of plenty. There's the peaceful stillness of cool autumn evenings & fresh Kaimoana on a stony beach, finished by the mouth-poppingly bright stars of the milky way. New Zealand Riesling is its landscape."
Angela Clifford - Tongue In Groove Wines and Riesling Girl

Notable examples include: Ata Rangi "Craighall", Babich, Mission, Palliser Estate, Dry River, Craggy Range "Te Muna", Astrolabe, Framingham, Fromm, Forrest, Greenhough, Grove Mill, Huia, Johanneshof, Kusuda, Lawson's, Little Beauty, Seresin Estate, Spy Valley "Envoy", Te Whare Ra, Villa Maria, Neudorf, Waimea, Black Estate, Pegasus Bay, Muddy Water (now owned by Greystone Vineyards), Waipara West, Carrick, Felton Road, Misha's Vineyard, Mt Difficulty, Pasquale, Peregrine, Prophet's Rock, Rippon and Valli amongst many others.

Pinot Gris

Kiwis tend to call it Pinot Gris instead of Pinot Grigio. Yes, they are the same grapes! Stylistically, the New Zealand wine style is more aromatic and similar to the Alsatian Pinot Gris, to which they aspire. Typically they display that pear, quince and stone fruit character and flavour profile. As with everything it is a question of balance. Pinot Gris is quite a prolific grape and given half the chance would grow just about anywhere, hence it has to be tamed, coaxed and managed properly. The key here is the equilibrium between naturally ripe sugars and phenolics in the grape, which produces an elegant wine with good palate texture and weight, yet also balanced with lovely fresh acidity. It is quite typical now for a Kiwi Pinot Gris to reach 14.5% and the tendency for wine makers is to refrain from the use of oak. Speaking as a sommelier, I believe Pinot Gris is a very food-friendly and versatile wine style. For instance, you may discover some which you can just drink on their own and are very fruit-driven and then there are others which display more aromatics and would be great partners with food. In my opinion, once you have got to grips with Kiwi savvy and you know you like it, develop your palate onto a Riesling or Pinot Gris. You'll never look back.

Notable examples include: Matakana, Takatu, Podere Crisci, Vin Alto, Bilancia, Dry River, Gladstone Vineyard, Urlar, Ant Moore, Astrolabe, Greywacke, Huia, Invivo, Little Beauty, Staete Landt, Wairau River, Villa Maria, Yealands Estate, Akarua, Amisfield, Chard Farm, Gibbston Valley, Mt Difficulty, Michelle Richardson, Ostler, Pasquale and Quartz Reef.

"Putting Pinot Gris is oak is like putting lipstick on a cow"
Mike Tiller - Owner Isabel Estate, Marlborough

Sauvignon Gris

An emerging grape variety and wine style currently pioneered in New Zealand by Brancott Estate, Sauvignon Gris is an original Frebch grape, although it's relatively similar to Sauvignon Blanc it has not made the same impact as its more noble cousin. Let's what and see...

Gewurztraminer

As with the previous two, this aromatic grape variety is on the up in New Zealand. Again, the Kiwis look towards Alsace for their inspiration and the wines display all those quintessential characteristics such as lychee, rose petals, Turkish delight, ginger and spice. Try them with a fragrant Thai curry or with seafood. In my opinion, the best one is produced by Nick Nobilo at Vinoptima "Ormond Vineyard" in Gisborne. Here, Gewurztraminer is the only wine he makes. Talk about putting all your wine eggs in one basket, eh? There are, however, some other good examples made in Martinborough, Marlborough, Nelson and Otago. One of my personal favourites is made at Lawson's Dry Hills in Marlborough. The late Ross Lawson was a real pioneer and a champion of Gewurztraminer. Their wine always does well in shows with its signature authentic style and for me it's the vineyard's liquid business card. Te Whare Ra, also in Marlborough and established in the late 1970s have some of the oldest Gewurztraminer vines in the region. Current owners Anna and Jason Flowerday have a real passion for aromatic white wines and are definitely worth discovering. Their old vines Riesling and Gewurztraminer also forms the main part of their white blend called 'Toru', which drinks really well with a spicy, seafood curry.

Notable other examples include: Stonecroft, Dry River, Forrest, Huia, Hunter's, Johanneshof, Little Beauty, Saint Clair, Spy Valley, Aotea, Seifried, Waimea, Misha's Vineyard, Pasquale and Rippon, amongst others.

Other aromatic white varietals:

Plantings of Viognier, Chenin Blanc, Pinot Blanc; Albarino, Arneis and Gruner Veltliner are increasing. In particular, look out for 'quirky' examples from Gisborne, Hawke's Bay and Marlborough, amongst other vineyard locations. Often these wines are made in limited quantities and so are only available at cellar door or in some exclusive restaurants.

I find these wine styles very interesting and I believe there is real potential here, especially to focus on their food-friendly qualities However, most of these experimental grape varities are only produced in relatively small quantities After all, it is very interesting to be able to make these innovative wine styles, but Sauvignon Blanc still remains the most widely-planted grape of all, with around three-quarters of New Zealand's grape production.

 "There's a lot of experimentation going on at the moment, especially with Arneis and Gruner Veltliner, which is really exciting. Things will take time, as it's still early days, yet Gisborne and Marlborough seem to be the places where it's at, as they do fruit really well." - Matt Thomson, wine maker.

This may be very well, however, I genuinely believe that New Zealand should limit their production of Gruner Veltliner. Yes, it's all very interesting and so on, but in my humble opinion they will NEVER produce a Gruner as good as the Austrians. Think about it, Austria is a land-locked country and has a continental climate and has the perfect conditions to make truly world class Gruner Veltliner wines that in turn have become the country's flagship variety.

In general, New Zealand has a maritime climate and is made up of two islands with extensive coastlines that are integral to the wine regions' personalities. I think therefore that New Zealand should focus their attention on Albarino. What's more, it's a grape variety that flourishes very well on maritime coastlines - look at northern Spain and Portugal, for instance and how Albarino works very well as a partner to seafood. Some of the world's best kaimoana is off New Zealand's shores. For me, it's a no-brainer.

Notable examples of other white aromatic varietals and blends include: Coopers Creek, Stanley Estates, Millton Estate, Esk Valley, Astrolabe, Sea Level, Mt Difficulty, Yealands Estate, Escarpment, Rock Ferry, Greenhough, Pyramid Valley, Elephant Hill, Churton, Hans Herzog, Staete Landt, Cambridge Road, Schubert, John Forrest Collection, Mountford Estate, Te Whare Ra, Seresin Estate, Wooing Tree, amongst others.

Chardonnay
Please forget about big, strapping Aussie Chardonnays of yesteryear with lashings of oak. Thankfully things have moved on a bit now and generally Kiwi Chardonnays tend to be less oaky, more subtle and elegant. The current trend is to favour fruit-driven styles, which are focused, expressive and less clumsy. Most of New Zealand's Chardonnay comes from the sunny region of Gisborne, which produces approachable, easy-drinking and inoffensive wines of good quality. In my opinion, within certain regions, such as Auckland, Hawke's Bay, Martinborough, Nelson and Central Otago, some of the Chardonnays have the potential to be world class and can proudly stand up alongside their iconic rivals from Burgundy and elsewhere. The taste and flavours

can range from citrus, through melon to full-on tropical fruit. A few of them are more serious, leesy and complex. In the hands of a talented viticulturist and wine maker, some of them are quite memorable, multi-layered and beautiful masterpieces. Moreover, some wine makers have learned their craft in Burgundy and are employing all these techniques in New Zealand. A greater understanding of using the right clones, making a few critical improvements, such as lees-stirring, which develops layers of texture and complexity and calming down the oak regime is definitely being put into practice.

Notable examples include: Goldwater "Zell", Man O'War "Valhalla", Kumeu River "Mate's Vineyard", Kumeu River "Coddington Vineyard", Villa Maria Single Vineyard "Ihumatao", C J Pask "Declaration", Clearview Reserve, Craggy Range "Kidnappers", Craggy Range "Les Beaux Cailloux" (n.b no longer made), Morton Estate "Coniglio", Sacred Hill "Riflemans", Trinity Hill, Ata Rangi "Craighall", Dry River, Kupe by Escarpment, Te Kairanga, Fromm, Giesen "Fuder" Single Vineyard, Mahi, Dog Point, Seresin "Reserve", Neudorf "Moutere", Bell Hill, Mountford, Pegasus Bay "Virtuoso", Pyramid Valley, Felton Road and Gibbston Valley Reserve "China Terrace", amongst many others.

A handful of New Zealand vineyards are also producing some interesting sparkling wines (in the 'traditional method'). However, please note that you should never call them "Champagnes", as that would be a vinous crime.

Notable examples include: Cloudy Bay "Pelorus", Daniel Le Brun, Forrest, Huia, Hunter's "Miru Miru", Morton Estate, Nautilus, No.1 Family Estate, Rock Ferry and Quartz Reef, amongst others.

Stickies have thankfully made it back into the UK. I will let you into a secret: on that first trip in 2001, I 'smuggled' more than six bottles of 'limited edition' dessert wines through customs in my suitcase!

Notable examples include: Dry River, Palliser Estate, Cloudy Bay, Framingham, Forrest, Fromm, Isabel Estate, Seresin, Stanley Estate, Seifried, Pegasus Bay and Villa Maria, amongst others.

Pinot Noir

Have you ever seen that famous wine road trip movie called "Sideways"? Two guys gallivanting around California quenching their thirst and searching for the ultimate wine. Look what it did for Pinot Noir. Allegedly, the sad old Merlot grape took a bit of a slamming. Like most wine lovers, connoisseurs and probably the majority of wine makers, Pinot Noir is my favourite wine style. In fact, we are all probably searching for the "Holy Grail" that is the ultimate Pinot Noir. For most people, including myself, the most quintessential example of this fickle grape comes from Burgundy in France. New Zealand is now producing some excellent quality Pinot Noirs. Yes, of course, the vineyards are many years younger and the wine makers have not been producing it for many generations, yet some of the best Kiwi wine makers have spent time and gained valuable experience with some of the best in the world. They have cut their vinous teeth, honed their craft and learned all the techniques necessary and then have applied them to their own land. The oldest Pinot Noir vineyards date back to the late 1970s and early 1980s. These vines are now at optimum age and are producing delicious fruit. I wholeheartedly encourage you to discover a Kiwi Pinot. The established vineyards are located within Martinborough, yet in certain parts of Marlborough, especially within the Brancott, Omaka and Waihopai Valleys they are making some good examples. Central Otago right down in the bottom of the South Island, near to Queenstown, is considered to be the new kid on the block and many vineyards are developing at a rapid rate with exciting results. For me, the small region of Waipara, just north of Christchurch is the most underrated wine region. Marlborough Pinots are just starting to get on peoples' wine radars too. Some of them are exquisite and could justly challenge the premier league Pinots from other regions. Although, I would urge any 'Pinotphile' to make a 'pilgrimage' to Wellington and discover the delights of the iconic wines of Martinborough.

Notable examples include: Ata Rangi, Cambridge Road, Craggy Range "Te Muna", Dry River, Escarpment (especially Kupe and Kiwa vineyards), Gladstone Vineyard, Julicher, Kusuda, Margrain, Martinborough Vineyards, Palliser Estate, Schubert, Te Kairanga, Urlar, Ara, Clos Henri, Delta Vineyard, Dog Point, Fromm "La Strada" and "Clayvin Vineyard",

Eaton Family Vineyards, Giesen Single Vineyard "Clayvin", Lawson's, Mahi, Nautilus, Saint Clair, Seresin Estate (especially Sun and Moon and Raupo Creek vineyards), Terravin Hillside Reserve, Villa Maria, Neudorf "Moutere" and "Tom's Block", Greenhough "Hope Vineyard", Black Estate, Pegasus Bay, Muddy Water (now owned by Greystone Vineyard), Daniel Schuster (unfortunately declared bankrupt), Mountford, Bell Hill, Pyramid Valley, Tongue In Groove, Felton Road, Cornish Point, Craggy Range "Zebra", Akarua, Amisfield, Bald Hills, Carrick, Chard Farm, Burn Cottage, Gibbston Valley Reserve, Judge Rock, Maude, Michelle Richardson, Mount Edward, Mt Difficulty, Misha's Vineyard, Olssen's (now known as Terra Sancta), Ostler, Peregrine, Quartz Reef, Rippon Vineyard, Surveyor Thomson, Tarras, Two Paddocks, Valli, Wild Earth and Wooing Tree.

Bordeaux Blends (Cabernet Sauvignon; Cabernet Franc; Merlot and Malbec)

To be completely honest, I am not really a Cabernet person. We all know that taste is very personal and when it comes to red wine, my preferences are for Pinot Noir and Syrah, although I have come to appreciate a very well-made bottle of claret in my time. Within New Zealand, distinctive micro-climates and soils are producing world-class wines. Most importantly this is down to the well-drained, gravel soils on which Cabernet thrives.

For great, well-structured Kiwi Bordeaux Blends, look no further than Waiheke Island and Hawke's Bay (Gimblett Gravels). There's something quite special about these two regions in the North Island that makes arguably the finest Bordeaux-style reds. Many of the vineyards, especially centred around Hastings, Napier and Havelock North in Hawke's Bay were established a long time ago. In fact the oldest winery in New Zealand is Mission Estate which was founded in Taradale in 1851. The leading wineries of Hawke's Bay, now mainly located on rich, alluvial, old riverbed soils such as Te Mata, Trinity Hill, Craggy Range, Esk Valley and Vidal co-exist with newer and more modern wineries. With a flurry of excellent recent vintages, Hawke's Bay is an exciting place to be. Over the years my palate has improved and I have come to appreciate the elegant, yet generously-structured reds that New Zealand has to offer

Notable examples include: Stonyridge "Larose", Goldwater "Esslin", Man O'War "Ironclad", Obsidian, Te Mata "Coleraine", Te Mata "Awatea", Trinity Hill, CJ Pask, Church Road, Esk Valley, Unison, Craggy Range "Te Kahu" and "Sophia", Sacred Hill, Forrest/Cornerstone and Te Awa.

Syrah

As you can see firstly Kiwis prefer to call it Syrah. The wine makers prefer to produce a Syrah, which tends to be more akin to the European styles than the Shiraz of their Aussie neighbours. Hence, they really aspire to the Rhone Valley in France. The wines tend to be more elegant and peppery with savoury, spicy black fruits than the powerful blockbusters of the Barossa Valley and McLaren Vale. Syrah can also take a little heat in warmer micro-climates, such as Waiheke Island and Hawke's Bay. Moreover, combined with the Gimblett Gravels soils, especially within the latter region, well-structured and flavoursome wines with great potential are being produced as a result. Do not overlook the cooler climate styles of Syrah from Martinborough and Marlborough too as they are wines to watch, although produced in a slightly different style. Notable examples include: Man O'War "Dreadnought", Te Mata "Bullnose", Bilancia "La Collina", CJ Pask "Declaration", Craggy Range "Block 14", Craggy Range "Le Sol", Stonecroft, Trinity Hill "Homage", Bridge Pa, Vidal, Forrest, Elephant Hill, Kidnappers Cliffs, Te Awa, Cambridge Road, Dry River, Martinborough Vineyards, Murdoch James, Schubert, Fromm, Staete Landt. and Te Whare Ra

Other red varieties:

Montepulciano, Tempranillo and Zinfandel, amongst other esoteric grapes and blends are becoming more popular too and are worth seeking out. N.B. many of them are made in very small quantites.

Here is a quick and simple recipe, which from time to time I like to cook, with a wine pairing. They perfectly encapsulate the tastes and flavours of New Zealand in a bowl and in the glass.

Asian noodle soup with prawns

—500ml chicken stock
—2 garlic cloves, peeled and sliced
—1 small knob of fresh ginger, peeled and finely grated
—1 teaspoon chilli flakes
—1 tablespoon sweet chilli sauce
—1 tablespoon dark soy sauce
—1 tablespoon oyster sauce
—½ teaspoon sesame oil
—Pinch of salt (optional)
—200g dried soba noodles or instant rice noodles (or regular noodles if you prefer)
—10-12 whole prawns, peeled
—2 heads pak choy, cut into quarters
—1 red chilli, sliced
—½ bunch coriander, chopped
3 spring onions, trimmed and finely sliced
1 lime, zested and cut into wedges

The key to a good flavoursome soup is a good stock so the first job is to make it big and bold. Pour the stock into a saucepan and place on a high heat. Of course, if you are a vegetarian then use a vegetable stock, but I prefer the flavour of chicken stock. Add the remaining aromatic ingredients and allow the broth to come to the boil. Taste to check the seasoning and that you are happy with the salt/spicy balance. Remember everyone has their own personal taste.

Add the noodles and the prawns and cook for around 4 minutes until the noodles are cooked through. At this stage add some coconut milk (optional), which will make the broth more fragrant and creamy and with a bit more texture as it reduces. Fold the pak choy into the broth and cook until the leaves are tender and the stalk still remains crunchy (about 2-3 minutes). Add the lime zest.

Serve in deep, warm soup bowls and sprinkle the sliced chilli, coriander and spring onions on top. Squeeze the fresh lime at the last moment for maximum zingy freshness.

Wine suggestion: the award-winning 2010 Little Beauty "Limited Edition" Dry Riesling, Marlborough. Wine maker: Eveline Fraser.

This wine was awarded "Best Riesling under £15" at the prestigious 2013 Decanter World Wine Awards.

"Acidity is the electric spark that ignites a wine. Most sommeliers are acid freaks: they favour wines with high acidity because acid lifts and frames most food."

Rajat Parr- sommelier and wine communicator

For more information on grape varieties and wine styles, please scan QR code with your smartphone.

"I'm just sitting here drinking some wine, eating some cheese and catching some rays! You know..."

Donald Sutherland - playing the character of "Oddball" in the movie "Kelly's Heroes" 1970.

NORTHLAND

NORTHLAND

As the name suggests, we will start off this road trip in the country's most northerly region. Most people, myself included, whenever they travel to New Zealand will touch down in the international city of Auckland. As we shall discover later on, not only does this cosmopolitan city have much to offer, but also is a great location to use as a base from which to travel. Most visitors to Northland arrive by car. Kerikeri, Whangarei and Kaitaia all have airports and there are regular flights from Auckland, but a car is essential for touring the region. The northern tip of New Zealand reaches out into the South Pacific in a long narrow finger that begins in South Auckland, passes through the city itself and its narrow isthmus of dormant and extinct volcanoes, then widens out into a knuckle that encompasses Hokianga in the west and the Bay of Islands in the east, and narrows again as it runs up Ninety Mile Beach to North Cape. The climate is distinctly balmy and tropical for most of the year. Miles of unspoilt coastline, large tracts of native bush dominated by magnificent kauri trees and the many sheltered harbours from Whangarei to Cape Reinga make this an ideal playground and tourist destination, especially lovers of golf, fishing and yachting.

The true birthplace of New Zealand wine, Northland reaches back to plantings in 1819 at Kerikeri by missionary Samuel Marsden. The first British resident, James Busby, made the first wines in this region. Only a handful of vineyards and wineries can be found there now, but a growing awareness of possibilities for the industry has brought new growers and wineries to the far north. For it is very challenging for the wine maker, especially to contend with the region's warmer micro-climate and humidity. Chardonnay and big bold reds are proving to be the most successful. For instance, it is far too tropical for the more delicate Pinot Noir grape. Northland is probably not the region that most people would choose to plant grapes for 'premium' wines given such adverse conditions. However, the very talented Mario Vuletich at Longview Estate is fiercely committed to the area and proud of the wines he and his wife produce from their vineyard south of Whangarei.

The climate is almost Mediterranean and therefore very suitable for growing fruits and vegetables, including olives and nuts. The cuisine, with its fresh produce, fish and seafood and a variety of tastes and flavours, has a distinctly more Mediterranean and pan-Asian influence as a result. All of these local ingredients and produce are available at the fabulous farmers' markets within the region. Must visits are Marsden Estate in Kerikeri, which is popular with the locals and Karikari Estate on the Karikari Peninsula, which features local produce and wines in their fabulous restaurant on a spectacular site overlooking the coast. The region boasts some of the country's top resorts and golf clubs, including Carrington and The Lodge at Kauri Cliffs. During my 2006 road trip, I met Fric Denis, a suave Frenchman, who was working as sommelier at the latter establishment. While touring around we visited some vineyards together, exchanged various tales and it was fun.

I have included Matakana within this chapter, even though for some it could be classified as North Auckland. It is just an hour's drive north of the city and has become a bit of a travel 'mecca' for most Aucklanders who enjoy its fine beaches and warm hospitality. Warkworth and Takapuna provide you with delightful pit-stops and stop-overs to break up your journey. Matakana also offers the best of rural New Zealand. The region is famed for its local produce and you will be able to taste and discover these at their fabulous farmers' markets and delicatessens. The regional wines are not too shabby either. A particular favourite of mine is the boutique vineyard called Takatu. There are now around 20 established vineyards in the region, at least half a dozen of which are open seven days a week for wine tasting and have cellar doors. Moreover, most of the vineyards have excellent restaurants with the delicious local produce on their menus. Matakana has the potential to produce top quality Pinot Gris and Bordeaux reds. It would certainly be worthwhile to spend a 'day trip' to visit the region and/or to join one of the various wine trails hosted by a local expert. My recommendations include: Ascension Vineyard, Heron's Flight, Hyperion, Matakana Estate (currently under administration) and Takatu.

TOP THINGS FOR YOUR "MUST DO" LIST:
Beaches, especially Ninety-Mile Beach
Cape Reinga
Bay of Islands
Farmers' markets
Golf courses and resorts

Please note: there is a whole host of information in the index at the back of this book.

"I guess like any country the local cuisine is often best paired with local wines. The challenge for New Zealand however is defining our cuisine - it is diverse and often a fusion of French, European, Asian and Pacific Rim flavours. Our wines pair well with many dishes , because both carry a theme of freshness, packed with distinctive flavours and textures. Our wines seem to weave in and around the food easily."

Cameron Douglas MS - Auckland-based Master Sommelier, wine consultant and sommelier mentor

GREATER AUCKLAND

GREATER AUCKLAND

Auckland is New Zealand's largest city with a population of more than one million people. As the city is regarded by most as the international gateway to the country, Auckland is probably the first place which the traveller will reach and the journey throughout New Zealand will normally continue from there. 2001 was the first time I visited New Zealand and I stopped off in the city for a few days with my sister after making the long-haul flight across the Pacific Ocean from Los Angeles. One small tip for you: crossing the International Date Line really throws you off course. When you touch down into Auckland, it is a short drive via motorway from Mangere, where the international airport is located, through the suburbs of South Auckland up to the city itself. After a while you will begin to see the urban sprawl, various neighbourhoods and the city's prominent landmark of the needle-shaped Sky Tower in the distance. The main routes which will take you into the CBD are Dominion Road and Queen Street. Auckland has a bit of a traffic problem so do not say I did not warn you.

As I explained earlier, I have always had an affinity with the country and my main reasons for visiting New Zealand were family and the love of a good woman. With regards to the latter, I have always regarded Sandy, the beautiful person I met in early 2000 in London as my true love and soul-mate. It was so nice to be able to see her again. I have returned to Auckland on many occasions and my loyal friend also helped me get over my personal tragedies and provided me with much comfort. I cherish her love and friendship very much and have some very happy memories of spending time with her. For instance, during 2005 I endured some horrible personal set backs and traumas, including the death of my loving Nonna and I just had to get away. I was also battling against mental illness and depression. At one point, I actually felt suicidal and I still haven't managed to get over those awful moments. New Zealand, over the other side of the world seemed the perfect bolt-hole to take a bit of time out, clear the mind, and to refresh and re-energise. So in March 2006 I left my job at Harvey Nichols, where I worked with some great people in a wonderful environment, and went on a six-month sabbatical. I am so glad I made that tough decision and luckily I had a very understanding boss – Paul Finucane at Harvey Nichols. I seriously believe that in life, love and work: timing is everything.

Rest assured, as I have visited Auckland on four occasions, this chapter will be packed with evocative anecdotes and highlights of my many experiences. Ever since 1999, Auckland has been known as "The City of Sails" and at the Viaduct Basin, home of the Americas Cup, visitors can have their fill of the nautical ambience and enjoy some wonderful bars, restaurants and cafés. Here my favourites include: Soul, Euro, Cin Cin on the Quay, Wildfire and the Hilton Hotel, located right at the end of the main wharf, with its swanky bar and restaurant. I enjoyed lovely meals with Sandy in all of those places, yet my favourite experience at the Viaduct Harbour was slurping on many feijoa martini cocktails, big fat oysters and sipping on Champagne at "White" restaurant overlooking the beautiful bay.

Auckland's cuisine is definitely Pacific Rim, with a few Mediterranean influences too. There is a large Asian community in the city, mostly Korean, whose culture and street food have been absorbed into the way of life. In many of the suburbs and especially along Queen Street and Karangahape Road (a.k.a "K Rd") you will find lots of noodle bars, take aways and so on. This city has it all. My favourite restaurant is probably O'Connell Street Bistro. This establishment has a great wine list which is very extensive. On the topic of wine – check out the small wine bar called Merlot just up the road. I was there a few years ago and they served a good selection of wines, especially by the glass with simple platters of tasty bites. With regards the weather – be prepared for "Four Seasons in one day".

Whilst in Auckland, I would suggest that you visit the two suburbs called Parnell and Ponsonby/Herne Bay. The latter has some great restaurants (my favourite being Vinnie's) and some lovely cafés and markets too. This neighbourhood is also home to Allpress Coffee Roasters (who have branches in London)and the vibe is similar to Islington. Ponsonby Road is the place to hang out, enjoy a cup of great coffee, have brunch and just watch the world go by. Parnell, on the other hand is just as trendy, yet has a similar ambience to London's Notting Hill with its boutiques, art galleries, café culture and restaurants. Sandy and I had an exquisite meal at Antoine's Restaurant. The chef there is regarded as one of the best in the city and the long-established restaurant itself is still going strong after many years. Within Auckland, allegedly Antoine's has a similar reputation to that of Le Gavroche in London. The cuisine at Antoine's is classic French-inspired- great quality, but given its own unique twist. I enjoyed a lovely lunch with my cousin Lucy and her partner (now husband) Andrew at Hammerheads, which is a fish restaurant out in one of the bays on the outskirts of the city along Tamaki Drive. The fresh tuna, swordfish and hapuku steaks are the dishes to go for. The markets in Victoria Park, the nearby fish market and Avondale farmers' market are also definite must-visits. We went there very early in the morning with Sandy's sister Bev and we saw heaps of fruits and vegetables, such as aubergines, taro, kumara, ginger and exotic herbs and spices. Situated in South Auckland, Avondale market is frequented by many local Maori and Asian people too.

Auckland is a great city to use as a base, from which to travel around the region. You can even do a bungy off the Sky Tower if you so wish. I will let you into a secret: I suffer from vertigo and in 2003 whilst in the city, I plucked up the courage to do one off the side of the tall tower. It obviously did not cure me of my fear of heights as I am still scared! For a more tranquil environment with less adrenalin-packed activities I suggest you head over to Kelly Tarlton's Water World on Tamaki Drive. Speaking of water, you can catch ferries from the harbour side downtown which will take you across to Devonport on the city's North Shore and beyond. From here, you can also get to Waiheke Island and take an excursion around the Hauraki Gulf and Great Barrier Island.

Fullers operate many regular and daily ferries from Auckland quayside and the ferry terminal to many destinations.

Waiheke Island has become the premier destination of Aucklanders for weekend retreats from the city and day trips to taste wine and the unspoilt beaches. Such is the demand for accommodation that the increase in building new residences on Waiheke now almost equals the rate of construction in downtown Auckland. Just a 40-minute trip in the fast ferry over the relatively-calm waters of the inner harbour, it is a world away from the frenetic urban pace. Visitors are immediately plunged into the 'island time' atmosphere. A few people have their holiday homes (bach) on the island or have chosen to live there and commute to work each day to Auckland. Once on the island it is very easy to get around, as shuttle buses meet the ferry to take arriving passengers to various destinations around the island. Alternatively, you can hire bikes and cars. A restaurant you should definitely check out is the newly-opened "Oyster House" where Cristian Hossack (ex-Head Chef at The Providores in London) is currently behind the stoves. If you do go there, you'll be in for a great meal experience.

Waiheke's reputation for powerful red wines was built on the original plantings and production of Stonyridge and Goldwater vineyards, but over the past 10 to 15 years many other vineyards have joined these pioneers, some of which are making equally rich and interesting wines. Visitors are welcomed at several wineries and can eat in good quality cafés. They can also choose from at least five luxury accommodation lodges. A favourite experience of mine on the island was having lunch on the veranda at Vino Vino, overlooking the beach down below with my sister, cousin Lucy and Sandy. I walked along the beach with Sandy and carved our initials into a nearby tree knowing I would return one day. The best views are from the fabulous Mudbrick vineyard restaurant. The wines are not too bad either, but their reputation is as a great venue for weddings, private functions and parties.

Goldwater Estate is the company that kick-started the Waiheke Island 'wine rush', yet today around 90 per cent of its grapes come from Marlborough. Though the total volume of wine produced from its Waiheke vineyards has now doubled, the Marlborough production (mainly for the Sauvignon Blanc) has increased at an even faster rate. I met Kim, Jeanette and their daughter, Gretchen and was shown around the vineyards (marked by the huge Pohutukawa tree up on the hill) by son-in-law and general manager Ken Christie. Even though they make excellent wines in Marlborough and now in Hawke's Bay, the company's flagship wines will remain its acclaimed Waiheke Island reds: Goldwater Esslin Merlot and Goldwater Cabernet Sauvignon. In addition, I am very fond of the bold and flavoursome Chardonnay from the Zell vineyard.

Whereas the Goldwater family established their vineyards on Waiheke in the early 1970s, the story of Stonyridge is a little different, yet its success has been perhaps even more dramatic. The singular vineyard is the source of what many consider to be New Zealand's greatest red wine – Stonyridge "Larose". Founder-owner Stephen White planted the vineyard in 1982 on land that was considered not much good for anything, and chose to name the wine after the rose because it represented the ultimate in "power, colour, beauty and bouquet". Cabernet Sauvignon is the principal grape in Larose, a wine which typically also contains Merlot, Cabernet Franc, Malbec and Petit Verdot. When I visited the vineyard, Stephen pointed out that Waiheke Island, like the Medoc in France's Bordeaux region, has a maritime climate in which Cabernet Sauvignon performs generally and consistently well. Growing all five classic Bordeaux varieties also gives you options and he shares the similar Bordelais philosophy of "not putting all your eggs in one basket." The island is also home to Te Motu vineyard, which is owned by the Dunleavy family. Terry Dunleavy was a former executive director of the New Zealand Wine Institute (formed in the 1970s) and currently he has left the running of the vineyard and winery business to his two sons. I enjoyed a delicious lunch at their "The Shed at Te Motu" winery restaurant and a glass or two of their wines.

Without question Waiheke Island has a place in New Zealand's vinous history, but there is one vineyard, of which I am a fan, that has hit the headlines and has been received much acclaim. Man O'War is located in the Stony Batter part of Waiheke and even though it has gained a recent rise in prominence it actually has a long history. So what is the story with Man O'War? Sarah Fogarty who used to work for the winery will enlighten us: "It goes all the way back to 1769 when everything was 'discovered'. The Man O' War journey began with a special piece of land, which indeed has a deep history. Located at the Eastern end of the island, Man O' War is a stunning array of coastal hillsides with high cliffs and pristine beaches forming a ruggedly beautiful coastline. It was actually along this coastline that Captain James Cook came to anchor during his first voyage around New Zealand in 1769. Upon sighting the ancient stands of Kauri trees ashore, Cook noted in his journals that they would make ideal masts for his warships of the Royal Navy. Thus the name Man O' War was bestowed upon this unique land. With a desire to protect this treasured land's natural beauty and sense of history for future generations, the current family owners purchased the four contiguous farms that now form the 4,500 acres of Man O' War Vineyards in the early 1980s. For more than 200 years, transporting ourselves through this voyage of discovery, it has now been acknowledged that world class wines could be produced in this location. In fact, I am convinced that the wines from Waiheke Island, especially those suitable varietals and styles mentioned earlier do have the potential to be worthy of that lofty status. The Man O' War vines were planted in 1993 and today consist of 150 acres planted in almost 90 individual hillside parcels (blocks), each with a distinct soil profile and micro-climate."

For instance, on the island you have the particular volcanic and mineral soils of Stony Batter, which impart their character into the vines and the wines. Essentially, this is what the term 'terroir' means, which sometimes tends to be misunderstood or misused. Again, this completely reinforces the notion of a genuine sense of place. For what sets these wines apart from other 'New World' examples is that they are much more in the 'classic' European mould with restrained elegance, as opposed to sheer power, intensity and juicy ripe fruitiness of their Aussie counterparts. This is the case most of all with Syrah.

Our road trip around Greater Auckland will now take us to one of New Zealand's most historic centres of viticulture. Aucklanders whose memories of the 'wine trail out west' stretch back to the '60s and '70s will today be able to find sophistication and serious wines in the "NorWest" region. The ultra-dry reds, sweet sherries and ports of those early years have been left well behind. As the birthplace of New Zealand's commercial wine industry (see timeline in my introductory chapter), this area has particular significance. Many of the pioneering Dalmatians first settled here, and important names such as Babich, Brajkovich, Corban and Spence made wines that were the foundation stones of the country's modern wine industry. Visitors to this region can visit the Spence brothers' winery, Matua Valley (now internationally owned), where the first Sauvignon Blanc was introduced to New Zealand, and the Brajkovich family of Kumeu River Wines, who led the way internationally with their well-regarded Chardonnay. The wineries of this region have also had triumphs and well-deserved acclaim with Bordeaux-style reds, as well as their Pinot Gris and Chardonnay.

Two distinct wine areas to be found within this region to the north and west of Auckland. Growers and producers in the Kumeu/ Huapai district, which falls into Rodney County, have banded together in order to market themselves with a good wine trail map. Other wineries can be found in Henderson and the surrounding valleys. Both areas are well served with casual cafés, and several wineries offer restaurants or picnic areas, making it a worthwhile day trip from the city. The wine country experience really starts where the North-Western Motorway from central Auckland spills out into the rural region, overtaken by the urban sprawl of the Henderson area. Do not overlook Lincoln Road either, which still boasts a handful of wineries, including the historic Babich. I visited them in 2006 and am a big fan of their wines, especially the Riesling. Many of the wineries have charming rural settings accessible from the State Highway 16, and there is plenty to see and do. For those who would rather be driven, there is also a range of custom-made wine tours available and you can always get a bus to Kumeu/ Huapai from the city. The vineyards which I visited include Soljans, Coopers Creek, Nobilo and the legendary Mazuran's (which still continue to make fortified wines). My stand-out memory was during the time of the vintage harvest of 2006, when I spent three days with Michael Brajkovich MW at Kumeu River. Probably more than any other winery, Kumeu River and the Brajkovich family can take credit for the rebirth of West Auckland as a wine making region of significance. When other long-established West Auckland wineries such as Babich, Nobilo and Montana started planting vineyards in other regions in the 1970s and 1980s, Kumeu River stayed put. Though the heavy clay soils and humid climate were not ideal for grapes, family patriarch Maté Brajkovich (Michael's late father) insisted on fully testing the region's potential before joining the exodus. His persistence, combined with the viticultural and vinification techniques learned by Michael at Roseworthy College (who became New Zealand's first Master of Wine), paid off. Michael also cut his vigneron's teeth with the Moueix family at various properties in St Emilion and Pomerol in Bordeaux during the legendary 1982 vintage and assisted at Chateau Magdelaine in 1983.

Kumeu River Chardonnay, especially the 'iconic' "Maté's Vineyard", along with Cloudy Bay Sauvignon Blanc from Marlborough, was one of the New Zealand wines that made the wine world sit up and take notice in the late 1980s. When I was there during the vintage harvest of 2006, it was such a genuine treat to be able to spend some time picking the brains of the great man. I have never forgotten the big smile on Michael's face when we tucked into some juicy ripe Merlot grapes just harvested from the vineyard. "The 2006 harvest is absolutely perfect! It almost reminds me of the 1982 Bordeaux – perfect natural ripeness, juicy and delicious, yet still with plenty of freshness. It makes my job a lot easier when working with such healthy grapes". Michael took me on an interesting tour of the winery buildings, including showing me the processes and techniques he uses for malo-lactic fermentation with his Chardonnays. Back in the day, he created a completely revolutionary wine style and the benchmark to which most Kiwi wine makers aspire. Other highlights included when he took me around the iconic "Maté's Vineyard" – named in honour of his pioneering father and the "Coddington Vineyard" and other vineyards which are on the Waitakere Road. We ventured to the West Coast with its wild black volcanic sandy beaches, Kaipara harbour and the gannet colony at Muriwai.

Though toheroa, the region's most famous indigenous food, are no longer gathered, plenty of other shellfish are available, as well as honey, vegetables and, of course, fruit. Michael told me an interesting story about the local seafood delicacy which is no longer available, but if you went into a particular restaurant and asked the owner (possibly with a nudge and a wink) for the "shellfish soup special" then you would get those delicious things in a bowl. Unfortunately, I never got the chance to sample them, but they sounded amazing. I did have the opportunity to sit down and enjoy a meal with the Brajkovich family, headed by Melba and her other sons Milan, Paul and daughter Marijana, who are all involved in running the family business.

This part of Auckland has much to offer: not only culturally and gastronomically, but also historically. The rich countryside that sweeps away from Auckland's Southern Motorway is known for its lifestyle blocks, stud farms for the racing industry and polo, and a scattering of vineyards. Another excuse to head back to Mangere, apart from the international airport, of course, would be to visit the vast and modern facility owned by Villa Maria headed up by George Fistonich. Not only has the Villa Maria brand become internationally famous, but also George has mentored some of the country's most talented wine makers. Here, the chief wine maker responsible for the entire range is Alastair Maling MW and Villa Maria wines have won many international awards and accolades. To the south of the city, Clevedon, the tiny township at the area's centre, has several wine producers (more boutique, than on the grander scale of Villa Maria) and is the gateway to a pretty coastline fronting the Hauraki Gulf. This area is definitely a worthwhile stop off en route down south towards Waikato. Most of the wineries in the Clevedon area offer tastings by appointment and my strong recommendation would be to visit Vin Alto. The region also has some delightful produce, which is available at the various delicatessens and farmers' markets. I suggest going to "Clevedon Produce", which is a kind of Kiwi version of Secrett's Farm or Petersham Nurseries in our Home Counties, for a wide selection of seasonal fruit and vegetables.

Having sold their gourmet food-importing company, Margaret and Enzo Bettio are now devoting all their energy to their one-of-a-kind winery, Vin Alto, in the Clevedon Hills. Their winery, established around 25 years ago, has been rebuilt and extended, a tasting room, delicatessen, farm, olive groves, restaurant and wine museum added, and more vineyards planted. What sets Vin Alto apart from other Kiwi wineries (with the exception of Heron's Flight in Matakana and now Montana, Forrest and Coopers Creek, who also make some Arneis) is that the vineyards are planted mainly in Italian grapes, including Pinot Grigio, Nebbiolo, Sangiovese, Montepulciano, Barbera and Dolcetto. The winery also uses classical Italian wine making techniques, such as the air-drying of grapes to shrivel them, thus concentrating the flavour and sugar – the process used to make Amarone and Vin Santo. Their Pinot Grigio wines are completely different and very rich, well-structured complex and aromatic. Most of Vin Alto's reds, such as its "Super Tuscan" inspired Celaio, are blends, but the main grape variety which flows throughout is Montepulciano. Vin Alto wines deserve to be discovered, and I believe they are best enjoyed with food.

Our journey continues...

TOP THINGS FOR YOUR "MUST DO" LIST:
Visit the fabulous restaurants, bars and coffee shops Greater Auckland has to offer
Viaduct Harbour
Sailing and watersport activities
Ferry over to Devonport and Waiheke Island
Wine tours of the regional vineyards and wineries
Sky City and Tower
West Coast beaches
Victoria Park Market and various local farmers' markets
One Tree Hill
Auckland Domain and various other scenic parks

Please note: there is a whole host of information in the index at the back of this book.

"Wine is bottled poetry"
Robert Louis Stevenson

WAIKATO / BAY OF PLENTY

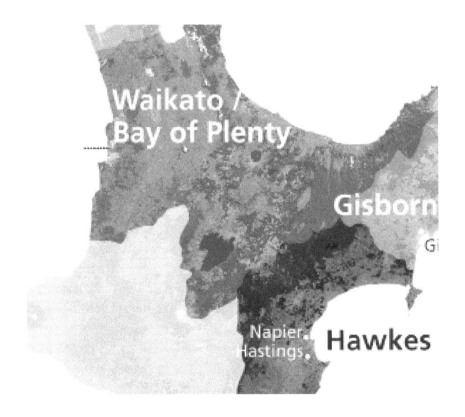

WAIKATO/BAY OF PLENTY

A car is essential for getting around here. When you drive south from the city of Auckland along the State Highway 1, through the Bombay Hills, you come to the region which is known as Waikato. In fact, New Zealanders call it "The Waikato" as it refers to the mighty river which flows out of Lake Taupo through much of the land and out into the sea just south of Pukehohe. My friend Sandy told me a wonderful story that at a young age school children are taught about the legendary river, which has a very important and historic significance in Maori folklore and culture. You may be interested to know that the region is the breeding ground of some of the finest racehorses in the world.

Hamilton, New Zealand's fifth largest city Is the capital of Waikato and is situated at a bit of a junction. To the north you have Paeroa (famous for its natural spring waters), Thames and the Coromandel Peninsula. This is a tourists' paradise and popular for those seeking a relaxing weekend retreat or an adventurous trek through the bush. Along the picturesque beaches and within the delightful bays and islands you will also discover some delicious oysters and mussels. Game-fishing and hunting are popular pastimes here too. This is also 'commune country' and many commune dwellers produce excellent honey and organically-grown produce. To the south, you have the coastal towns of Raglan and Kawhia and its historic harbour, the Waitomo Caves and the bountiful rural lands of the King Country and Taranaki. The locality is known for its fish, in particular the flounder and shellfish such as pipis. Much further south, Taranaki, with the mighty volcano as its centrepiece, is very agricultural and is well-known for its beef cattle and dairy produce. Further east along State Highway 2 you will encounter Tauranga and the Bay of Plenty and the popular destination of Rotorua. The Bay of Plenty, aptly named by Cook, is very fertile and agricultural, where fruit (particularly kiwi and citrus fruit) flourishes in the rolling countryside. The biggest urban area in the bay is Tauranga, a commercial harbour, which is also quickly developing as a resort centre. Further along the coast you will come to Te Puke and Whakatane.

Thermal activity is a feature of this entire region. Rotorua, at the heart of the volcanic Central Plateau, is one of the country's most popular and commercialised tourist resorts, with a range of large-scale attractions geared up towards the incoming busloads. The whole city seems shrouded in a steamy mist and bubbling with boiling mud pools. 2001 was the first time I went there with my sister and the sulphurous smell in "Roto-Vegas" (my cousin Lucy mentioned to us that is what the locals call it) was quite off-putting. I had a good time in Rotorua as we visited all the local attractions and we also celebrated New Years Eve there. We enjoyed a big juicy T-bone steak, which came topped with a fried egg in the hotel's restaurant located with a grandstand view of the Rotorua race course! The main thermal area within the boundaries of the city is the extensive Whakarewarewa, which features boiling mud pools, silica terraces, steam vents and other thermal phenomena. The main part of the reserve is the Geyser Flat, which has at least seven active geysers, including two which perform with almost clockwork reliability: the "Prince of Wales Feathers" and the mighty "Pohutu". Please note: watch out for the splashing, and do not say I did not warn you about the smell of rotten eggs!

The eleven lakes in the Rotorua district are rich in rainbow and brown trout, many reaching trophy proportions. The region is also a major centre for Maori art and culture, and talented jade and wood carvers continue to develop their work from a traditional base into sophisticated and modern designs. Further afield, out in the bush, there are also opportunities for lovers of wild produce and game. The region is noted for pheasants, wild mushrooms and truffles. So, in between inhaling the wafts of sulphur, you may be in the mood to get out into the "woop woops" and do a bit of hunter-gathering and foraging. My late grandfather Bob used to enjoy a bit of game shooting and I am sure he would have been a very happy bunny in the bush with shotgun in hand and loyal dog by his side.

Of course, with good food you need good wine. A handful of wineries welcome visitors in this fertile dairy region. Tauranga, the area's major tourist destination (apart from Roto-Vegas and the Tongariro National Park), includes Mills Reef Winery, and nearby Katikati is home to Morton Estate. Both of these have excellent winery restaurants. A great deal of attention has been devoted to the match between the Morton Estate wines and the food at the estate's restaurant. Morton Estate is perhaps most well known for its iconic Black Label Hawke's Bay Chardonnay, long considered a benchmark of excellence. But the company's 'pinnacle' wine is "Coniglio" – quite a highly-regarded wine, hence priced appropriately and is an even more rarefied Chardonnay that had the distinction of being New Zealand's most expensive when it was launched in 2001. Both wines are sourced from the cool, elevated Riverview Vineyard at Mangatahi.

TOP THINGS FOR YOUR "MUST DO" LIST:
Coromandel Peninsula
White Island
Waitomo Caves
Whakarewarewa Maori Village in Rotorua

Please note: there is a whole host of information in the index at the back of this book.

"Wine is sunlight gathered"
Galileo.

GISBORNE

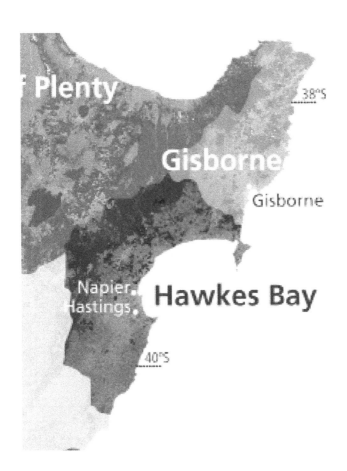

GISBORNE

As signs welcoming you to Gisborne testify, its biggest success story is cool, crisp Chardonnays, delicious when served with the local crayfish. Think of food in this area and picture shellfish – tuatua, pipi, mussels and paua. But food was not always plentiful here. In 1769 Captain Cook moored the Endeavour near what is now Gisborne and sent some of his crew ashore to find supplies. When they returned almost empty-handed he named the area Poverty Bay, and after skirmishes that left six Maori dead he sailed north around the cape to where pork and kumara were in abundance, anchoring in what he dubbed the Bay of Plenty.

As the most easterly of the country's wine regions, Gisborne is first to see sunlight each day. There is plenty of it to be seen in this relatively unspoilt area, making it a great tourist destination. Its hospitable wine trail is a delight for the adventurous and those prepared to make appointments to meet wine makers. Several operators offer custom tours tailored to individuals or groups. Gisborne's balmy climate is suitable for growing Chardonnay (more than a quarter of New Zealand's Chardonnay vines is planted here) and other white varietals that exhibit full fruit flavours. At present, there is a great deal of potential here to improve on quality and much experimentation is going on with grape varieties such as Viognier, Chenin Blanc and Arneis. In fact, grapes have been grown in the area since the first recorded plantings at Manutuke in the 1850s, and Montana (now Brancott Estate) has led the way with modern varietals by growing Chardonnay vines on the 'flats' that surround the city for the past thirty-odd years. This company and other pioneers, such as Matawhero and Millton Estate, have together put this area firmly on the world wine map.

To be honest, not visiting Millton Estate vineyards whilst in Gisborne could be considered committing a vinous crime. James and Annie Millton are passionate about their biodynamic winery and welcome visitors by appointment. In fact, a more passionate couple in wine I have not yet encountered.

There is always an exception to every rule – or, in the case of Millton Vineyard, there are two. Conventional wisdom has it that Poverty Bay is unsuited to the production of either Riesling or Pinot Noir, being too warm and wet. But the couple at their Manutuke winery consistently produces fine examples – "Opou Vineyard" Riesling and "Clos Ste Anne Naboth's Vineyard" Pinot Noir.

One of my best memories of travelling around New Zealand was having the opportunity to meet them and tread the hallowed soils of their well-cared-for vineyards. I have been a big fan of their wines for many years and used to serve them at Orrery Restaurant in Marylebone. In June 2011, I presented two of the Millton Estate wines at my "Craving for Chenin" pop up blind tasting in London, which included a selection of 40 Chenin Blancs from around the world. In my humble opinion, the "Te Arai Vineyard" Chenin Blanc can stand side by side as equals with the great revered wines of the Loire Valley. Tasting notes, comments and a full line up of the wines are available on my website and there is a link towards it in the index section.

"In 1984 they thought we were crazy to grow our grapes organically. We've spent the last twenty-five years proving that they were right! Now, it seems everybody wants to be crazy, and that's just what this planet needs. Crazy by Nature – makes perfect sense. We are one of the first winegrowers in the Southern Hemisphere to practice the use of biodynamic techniques in the vineyard and cellar. We've learnt that if you are kind to Nature she will always repay you, with quality. We try and build a balance; to create harmony so that there will be no place for "disease". It's no secret that the best bottle of wine is made of grapes from a vine that has been grown with sensitivity to the environment. We use special herbal, mineral and animal preparations and don't use herbicide, insecticide, systemic fungicide or soluble fertiliser. The Te Arai vineyard is five kilometres from the sea. Te Arai roughly translates to "the place where you pause before going on towards the land of eternal sunshine." Quite appropriate for this wine, I thought. This maritime proximity underlies the wine's unique South Pacific style. The silt soils give fragrance while the occasional incidence of botrytis, generated by the autumnal mists from the Te Arai stream, give complex texture, body and a sense of sweetness to the wine. In the Loire Valley of France, Chenin Blanc produces powerful wines of a similar character, which we refer to as our touchstone."

James Millton – The Millton Estate Vineyard

Another one of my favourite wines from Gisborne is the Gewurztraminer made by the talented Nick Nobilo at Vinoptima. In fact this is the only wine style he produces at the ten hectare estate in Ormond. Nick's vision is simply to produce the world's best Gewurztraminer. He has long held the view that this aromatic grape, especially from Ormond can become recognised as being amongst the best of this wine style in the world. He has now turned his vision into reality with this unique wine. Latin for "best wines", Vinoptima is based on the French ethos of terroir and combines the best of both old and new world practices. Gisborne's slightly warmer microclimate and conditions are perfect for this grape variety. Vinoptima Gewurztraminer has genuinely become an iconic wine within New Zealand and will normally be found listed within the best restaurants and on the shelves of the finest wine merchants. Gisborne also seems to be the region that a few wine makers have chosen to experiment with esoteric grape varieties such as Gruner Veltliner and Arneis. Even though these wines are made in limited quantites, look out for them, as the results are already looking quite promising.

TOP THINGS FOR YOUR "MUST DO" LIST:
Wainui Beach
Te Urewera National Park
Lake Taupo

Please note: there is a whole host of information in the index at the back of this book.

HAWKE'S BAY

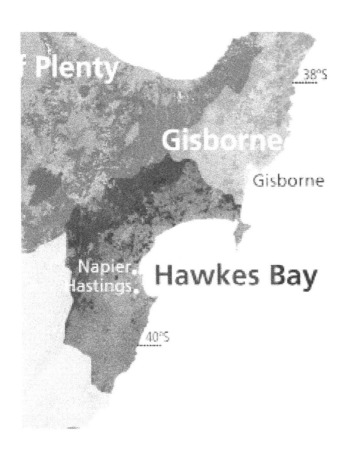

HAWKE'S BAY

Apart from tasting the 'usual suspects' from Marlborough, one of the first ever wines I tasted from New Zealand came from Hawke's Bay. If I remember rightly it was a red from Te Mata. I also have fond memories for the wines of CJ Pask and Trinity Hill, which I first encountered back in the early 1990s. How things have changed over the years, not only dramatically, but also thankfully for the better, as this region, in particular for its reds has the potential to be truly magnificent.

The wealth of gourmet treats to be discovered along the wine, food and art trails that weave their way through Napier, Hastings, Havelock North and the surrounding countryside certainly make this Hawke's Bay an exciting region to visit. I recommend that you spend quality time within the region, especially if you are an antiques buff, as Napier is a very cultural place, full of art deco and other treasures which I am sure will delight any connoisseur. In addition, to the west you have the central part of New Zealand which contains the spectacularly vast Lake Taupo. The produce from this region is varied and delicious and fine restaurants abound. Lake Taupo's fat trout are legendary, and if you catch one your lodge restaurant will often agree to cook it for you. Forget about BYO, now you can have BYOT! Rest assured, I have a simply exquisite recipe and wine pairing for you later.

The extensive Hawke's Bay Wine Country, as it has become known, covers an extensive area, taking in fertile plains and rolling hills, a broad sweep of spectacular coastline and the dominant Te Mata peak. Either way, if you get to the region by car or fly in on a domestic flight, consider this generous and bountiful region as a gastronomic pit-stop on your journey before heading south. In addition, it has a whole host of famous markets and more besides to discover and enjoy. Key operators within the region have helped awaken the community to wine tourism, with maps and touring ideas on offer at most wineries and from the region's information centres. Farmers' markets are held throughout the year, and this has stimulated growers and producers to make artisan products. Every weekend, locals and visitors throng to what must be the country's leading farmers' market, held at the Hawke's Bay Showgrounds. A smaller version is held in Napier and, from time to time, the tiny but dynamic Village Growers' Market takes up temporary residence in the Black Barn vineyard in Havelock North. A kind of 'pop up' farmers' market if you will.

The Hawke's Bay wines are highly regarded both locally and internationally and many have gone on to achieve iconic status. More than 30 local wine makers have banded together to market their "Gimblett Gravels" appellation, applied to wines produced from these unique soils of the area. Hawke's Bay's long, balmy summer gives the grapes plenty of time to develop rich flavours and a deep structure for longevity. Chardonnay and the red grape varietals, especially Cabernet Sauvignon, Merlot and Syrah have performed particularly well here. Many wineries have gone on to establish a connection with food, and a number of excellent winery restaurants serve seriously delicious fare. Plenty of fine wines can also be tasted at the cellar door. I have very fond memories and my recommendations include: Craggy Range, Te Mata, Bilancia, Unison, Trinity Hill, Esk Valley, Bridge Pa amongst others (all of which I have served during my time as a top-flight London sommelier at Oxo Tower, Fifth Floor at Harvey Nichols and Orrery).

Must visits and great sight-seeing while in the region include: Napier's world-renowned art deco buildings, Cape Kidnappers' gannet colony, exploration in the Te Awanga area, sheep-station tours and superb golf courses. "Hawke's Bay in a Glass" is also an amazing experience. As well as the iconic and prestigious names, including Stonecroft, Vidal, Mission Estate and Ngatarawa, which are part of the region's vinous heritage, you can also make some interesting discoveries with some more recent and up-and-coming vineyards such as Black Barn Vineyards, Elephant Hill, Hatton Estate, Kevern Walker, Lime Rock and Sacred Hill. These 'new kids on the block' are making some good wines, but great wines require a certain degree of patience. The Hawke's Bay reds, especially the Bordeaux-esque blends and deep, flavoursome Syrahs are generally noted for being very well-structured and having potential for long-ageing. I certainly hope your patience will be rewarded with a beautiful wine. A couple of years ago, I enjoyed a bottle of 1998 Te Mata "Awatea" red and it was perfect, yet still had potential for further development. What made it even better was that I had kept that particular bottle in my cellar for more than eight years.

For me though the real jewel in Hawke's Bay's crown is the Syrah. A pioneer of the Gimblett Gravels and a greatly respected boutique wine producer, Stonecroft founder Alan Limmer defines his aim as "to make wine where you don't have to read the label to know what you're drinking". In other words, varietal character is key. Alan planted his first vines in 1983 and experimented with many grape varieties before deciding he would concentrate on Syrah for his only red wine. He also produces Chardonnay and Gewurztraminer. Stonecroft is credited with making the first world-class New Zealand Syrah, and in the process confirming the Gimblett Gravels' suitability for that now highly fashionable wine style. Within New Zealand, Syrah is definitely 'on the up'.

The Kiwi version is definitely more European, inspired by the great Rhone examples, with its peppery and savoury flavour, compared to the richer and more voluptuous Shiraz wines of their Australian neighbours. In New Zealand, red grape varieties, including Bordeaux-esque and Syrah have enjoyed a string of good vintages since 2004, especially 2007 in Hawke's Bay. Syrah from the Gimblett Gravels in Hawke's Bay is one of the country's most exciting emerging styles. These astonishingly powerful, yet elegant wines have beaten the best from Australia and South Africa at the annual Tri Nations Wine Competition in five out of the last eight years. Let's see if the record will be better in the rugby! However, the most interesting and encouraging piece of information is that New Zealand produces these amazing wines from less than 300 hectares of Syrah vines. In contrast, Australia totals 45,000 ha and South Africa more than 8000 ha of Syrah/ Shiraz vineyards. Hawke's Bay, and especially its important sub-region and particular terroir of Gimblett Gravels seem to have stolen the show with regards to Syrah.

Whilst we're on the topic of terroir, not only is that the name of their iconic winery restaurant in Hawke's Bay, but also, in my view, Craggy Range is perhaps the New Zealand winery which exemplifies this concept to its fullest.

"Craggy Range began with two families who shared the same dream – to select and source the best land and vineyards in the country, and plant the vines perfectly suited to that terroir. To make wines which spoke more of the place they came from than any other, bottled as single estate wines. Finally – to have their wines listed in the world's great restaurants and fine wine merchants. Terry (TJ) Peabody and Steve Smith MW, sought for terroirs which would make their vision live. This is the legacy – born of those two families who lived the dream."

"Throughout Craggy Range there is a sense of the tradition of wine making. Natural methods protect the innate character and integrity of each parcel. But the sciences of viticulture and oenology are embraced when they're needed – such as in our state-of-the-art wine making facilities. But, in all stages – the art and skill of human hands play a sensitive and critical role".

With that last quote, you may think this just a load of marketing waffle, but I would encourage those sceptics amongst you to visit them and to see for yourself. For me, Hawke's Bay is definitely a region to enjoy and to watch in the future. Wine tourism has massive potential here. Craggy Range's "Les Beaux Cailloux" vineyard in Gimblett Gravels that produced the iconic Chardonnay has now been re-planted with Syrah - so let's see what happens here with future vintages. But for now, onwards and downwards in a southerly direction to the region of Wairarapa - New Zealand's 'spiritual home' of truly world class Pinot Noir.

TOP THINGS FOR YOUR "MUST DO" LIST:
Cape Kidnappers and Te Awanga
Fine Wine and Food Trail
Farmers' markets
Napier - famous for its Art Deco architecture and being a haven for antiques lovers

Please note: there is a whole host of information in the index at the back of this book.

"If I could give you New Zealand Pinot Noir on a piece of paper it would be a map to the things we treasure most, our people. This treasure map would help you find the 'crazies', the eccentrics, the magnanimous and hospitable. It would wind its way from the Waiarapa in the North to Central Otago in the South. Along the way you'd find those living the dream and those killing themselves to realise it. You'd come across noble, forgiving, fringe-dwelling romantics. There would be many un-realists and non-accountants, alternative thinkers and hedonists, food lovers and vine gardeners. Many would be decked out in outrageous garb. There would be endless rainbows around every corner and with them moving pots of gold. Here you would find the lovers, the dreamers and me."
Angela Clifford - Communications and Social Media for Pinot Noir 2013 - a bi-annual, international celebration of Pinot Noir held in the city of Wellington. For more details, please go to www.pinotnz.co.nz

WAIRARAPA

WAIRARAPA

As I explained earlier, my primary reason for travelling to Auckland was the love of a good woman. Family, food and wine also featured on the agenda and plenty of fun. However, my main reasons for travelling to the Wairarapa were definitely family and wine. For me the latter was almost a 'pilgrimage', especially to visit the great iconic vineyards located in Martinborough. The first time I went there was in 2001 when I made the long coach journey from Auckland with my sister via a stop over in "Roto-Vegas" and down through the centre of New Zealand's scenic North Island. The main route which takes you directly to the city of Wellington is the State Highway 1. It literally starts in the tip of the North Island and you drive through some dramatic landscapes, around the vast Lake Taupo, past the mighty Mt Ruapehu and other volcanoes, through Tongariro National Park, bypassing rural Taranaki and relatively-boring Palmie and down the pictur-esque Kapiti Coast. It was quite a "tiki tour" and must have taken around ten hours or so, including stop offs and 'comfort breaks' along the way. Of course, we could have taken the easy option and just flown down to Wellington, as my parents did a year earlier. It was a great way to see the country though and another option is to take the State Highway 2 via Hawke's Bay following the East Coast down to the Wairarapa region.

In 2001, a year after our parents' trip, my sister and I finally got the opportunity to meet our family in Wellington. First we spent time in Waikanae with Nancy and Fred, which was delightful. The coastline is picturesque and on a good day you can see right across to the South Island. Along the Kapiti Coast you have some quaint and tranquil towns - Levin, Otaki, Ohau (where a couple of vineyards are located), Lindale (home of Kapiti Cheeses), Parapa-raumu, (an international golf course) Paekakariki and so on – all of which are reminiscent of Sussex and Kent coastal towns with an ambience of somewhere such as Eastbourne. Coincidentally, that was the name of the Wellington suburb on Days Bay, where Fred and Nancy lived before moving to Waikanae.

Stand-out memories of time spent with my family include going up to Lindale to visit Kapiti Cheeses (my favourite is the Kikorangi Blue) and the Southward Car Museum with its vast array of classic and vintage cars. We enjoyed home-cooked meals together in their lovely house and wondered in amazement at their beautiful, well-kept garden filled with exotic flora. Uncle Fred must have been well into his 80s, yet was still young enough to have a computer hooked up in the back room to keep an eye on the internet. It was ideal because I could check my e mails and various appointments that I had lined up for vineyard visits in Martinborough. On one occasion, my uncle answered the phone and in the usual manner politely asked who was calling. The reply came: "It is Richard Riddeford from Palliser Estate. Tell Robert that we're expecting him to visit us!"

Ray and Lee came over to Waikanae to pick us up. After a sumptuous lunch, including Lee's legendary pavlova, they took us over the hills via Paekakariki to Upper Hutt where they lived. The views along the coastline and over to the South Island are stunning. My sister and I spent some time with them and they looked after us very well. On the first night we ate fish and chips from their local for supper. It was really lovely just to have a simple family meal together (with no airs and graces) out in their back garden. I was also impressed as Ray produced a bottle of Palliser Estate Riesling from the fridge to drink. Up until the previous year, my aunt and uncle had not really consumed much wine. However, that soon changed when my father met my uncle and perhaps a little bit of his knowledge and enthusiasm for the fermented grape juice rubbed off on him. With a little encouragement, my uncle soon became more aware of the wonderful wines which his country produced. I believe that every wine has a story and a situation which you remember for a reason. Straight forward as it was, for me that experience sitting down with family, enjoying fish and chips and a bottle of wine was truly memorable. I realised that Kiwis, even relative wine novices such as my uncle and aunt had no 'hang ups' about drinking Riesling either! I also got the impression that everyone served lamb shanks, big wedges of carrot cake and of course, pavlova. I returned to Upper Hutt the following year for seconds.

I have now visited Wellington on a few occasions. A huge harbour, steep hills and ferocious winds are the three defining physical characteristics of the nation's capital. It was probably its strategic position in relation to the South Island which prompted the New Zealand Company to choose Wellington as the site of its first settlement in 1840. In so doing, it successfully anticipated the colonial administration – which 25 years later moved the capital from Auckland to Wellington for that very reason, fearful that the inhabitants of the South Island might try to form a separate colony. Even to this day, a big rivalry between the North and South Islands, and indeed between Wellington, the country's capital and Auckland, the country's largest city still exists.

Today the 'harbour city' or 'windy city' lies partly on reclaimed land, with the original waterfront streets (such as Thorndon Quay and Lambton Quay) now high and dry in the middle of the central business district. Most of the compact downtown area (Te Aro) is flat, but the rest of the city climbs across the surrounding hillsides. I would suggest taking a ride on the Kelburn Cable Car up the steep hill from Lambton Quay downtown up to Kelburn Heights. The views from there and the Botanical gardens are spectacular. Great views of Port Nicholson (Wellington Harbour) and the bays are also afforded from Mt Victoria Lookout. The road is signposted from Oriental Bay and Courtney Place. From there I remember being able to see Petone and right up the Hutt Valley to Upper Hutt and beyond. Wellington may not be Auckland or Sydney, which both have the 'wow factor', yet on a good day its harbour is beautiful. Whilst in the city, must-visits also include the Museum of New Zealand Te Papa Tongarewa, the "Beehive", which contains the executive offices of Parliament and Old St Paul's Cathedral, which consecrated in 1866 and has a beautiful interior made entirely of native wood.

Wellington is a very cosmopolitan city and has a vibrant café culture and some fine restaurants. There is also a very good arts and music scene. The locals do not put up with bad coffee either. I have always enjoyed good experiences in Wellington. My recommendations would be Logan Brown and Shed 5, amongst others. The district known as Oriental Bay is also wonderful. A friend of mine, Daniel Primack from Around Wine in Marylebone, London visited Wellington back in the early "Noughties" and distinctly remembered a bar downtown called Good Luck Bar. He mentioned: "This place had an ambience of an old-fashioned speakeasy. We could have been in Chicago during the 1930s. I enjoyed myself drinking bourbon and listened to music all night long and had a lot of fun."

We drove over the Rimutaka Hill road which winds its way through the Rimutaka Ranges between Wellington and the Wairarapa plains. Martinborough has now become a huge destination for wine lovers, especially those who adore Pinot Noir. As I mentioned, I was in the process of making my pilgrimage to visit the area's great vineyards. Every two years the city of Wellington and the region plays host to the Pinot Noir Conference and there are many tastings and events which showcase the nation's very best wines and produce. Martinborough's fine wines, especially its top-notch Pinot Noirs, have made this region a must-visit on the Kiwi wine trail map. Early wine makers recognised the terroir of the Martinborough Terraces as ideal for vines, and their labours have been rewarded with international recognition. Back in the early 1980s, the original four pioneering wineries were Ata Rangi, Dry River, Chiffney and Martinborough Vineyards. Recent years have seen plantings escalate to the north and west of the original area and throughout the Wairarapa towards Masterton, Greytown and Carterton. So we braved the route over the hills and visited a couple of vineyards, including Palliser Estate and Martinborough Vineyards and then enjoyed a delightful lunch in the restaurant at the iconic Martinborough Hotel. Funnily enough the wine which we drank has escaped me, but I definitely remember we chomped our way through some amazing steaks. The restaurant's wine list is an oenophile's delight, and its pages are chock full of all the great and the good of Aotearoan wine aristocracy.

Martinborough is the town most visitors head for and the central area around The Square continues to develop, boasting excellent accommodation, several good restaurants, cheese-mongers, delicatessens and other food and wine-related businesses. I would suggest that you pop into the Martin-borough Wine Centre on Kitchener Street which focuses on the wines of the region, offering a full range of flights of tasters. The very knowledgeable staff will help you with your purchases. The Village Café is also a good pit-stop for a bite to eat. Standing proudly taking centre stage on The Square is the Martin-borough Hotel, which is an elegant, restored wooden building with individually themed rooms opening to verandas, balconies or courtyards in the town's heart. Allegedly, the place did not have such a salubrious reputation back in the day. Rosemary George MW would like to share a nice little anecdote: "The first time I went to Martinborough was way back in 1991. I visited the original four vineyards – Ata Rangi, Dry River, Chiffney's and Martinborough Vineyards. At the time, the wine maker of the latter was Larry McKenna. As I was a woman travelling on her own, I was booked into a local B & B, which afforded me all the homely comforts. However, I was lead to believe that the now-famous and swanky Martinborough Hotel did not enjoy such a lofty and salubrious reputation and would be therefore considered inappro-priate."

On re-visiting the region, I went to Ata Rangi and Dry River myself amongst other vineyards. Neil McCallum, wine maker at Dry River, whose wines have attained a virtual cult status, has a doctorate in chemistry from Oxford and takes an almost cerebral approach to his craft. Not only does he come across as being extremely fastidious, but also quite a shy, almost reclusive man. Before visiting his vineyards and winery you have to make an appointment. The sign above the entrance gate constantly says "CLOSED". You get the message of sheer exclusivity, which could be translated as a certain aloofness. Anyway, it was a

Sunday morning, I was there and I took the opportunity to call in. After all, I had come all the way from England to New Zealand and was only a few paces from this iconic vineyard and potentially going to meet a man held in very high esteem within the wine world. It was around midday, I knocked on the front door and Dr Neil McCallum opened it to be confronted by a complete stranger just staring at him. I recognised him immediately as I had seen photos of him in wine books. "I am very sorry to disturb you sir, but I just wanted to have the opportunity to meet you and shake your hand. I have been a big fan of your wines for many years." I said. Aware of this slight inconvenience and intrusion on his privacy, as he was just in preparation for Sunday lunch and had to deal with an unannounced visitor, I promptly made a sharp exit.

On the other hand, the experience at Ata Rangi was much more illuminating. Clive Paton of Ata Rangi is considered to be one of "The Three Wise Men of Martinborough Wine making". The other two are Larry McKenna (now Escarpment Vineyard) and Dr Neil McCallum. They are the most experienced of Martinborough's wine producers and among them they have produced some of the most distinguished wines of the region. For many years, Clive shared the wine making duties with Olly Masters (currently consulting at Seresin Estate in Marlborough and Misha's Vineyard in Central Otago). Even though the vineyard is noted for its Pinot Noirs and being acclaimed as one of the country's best examples, Ata Rangi also make excellent Chardonnay (Craighall and Petrie vineyards) and Pinot Gris (Lismore vineyard). However, one of my favourite wines which they produce is the "Celebre" which is a Bordeaux blend with a big dollop of peppery Syrah. The latter grape variety is showing big potential within the region and other wineries such as Murdoch James, Cambridge Road, Dry River and Schubert amongst others are making some interesting wines from it.

Two other favourite vineyards of mine are Martinborough Vineyards and Palliser Estate. The origins of Palliser Estate date back to the earliest days of winemaking in the region. At present

Palliser has the area's biggest output, with a large, but growth has not compromised its quality and consistency. The second label, Pencarrow, that rivals many producers' premium brands for quality, especially for its Sauvignon Blanc, is great value for money. In 2010 we enjoyed a silky smooth 2004 Palliser Estate Pinot Noir (a present from Uncle Ray to my father) with our family Christmas dinner.

Larry McKenna, formerly of Martinborough Vineyards, is considered to be one of the founding patriarchs of great Pinot Noir wine makers within New Zealand. He is actually an Aussie! I have met him on more than one occasion, most recently in London at the Escarpment dinner at The Providores and at the Martinborough Wine makers Pinot Noir tasting and lunch at Vinoteca. I have been a big fan of his wines for many years. The "Kupe" and "Kiwa" Pinots showed beautifully with the food and were real highlights. Great wines come from the heart and Larry McKenna strives and lives to produce great wine. It is that simple. A deep affinity for Pinot Noir, and passion for this "most challenging and capricious of grapes to grow and make good wine from", has driven him ever since. Outstanding wines speak of their own place, and Larry chooses Martinborough as the place to perfect his craft. Refreshingly open and straightforward in his approach, he values collaboration and has helped numerous workshops including many international Pinot Noir Conferences in New Zealand. He has also mentored and continues to mentor many wine makers, including Claire Mulholland (formerly at Martinborough Vineyards and who then went on to be wine maker at Amisfield in Central Otago).

In 1999 Larry felt it was time to rise to an irresistible challenge: creating a definitive New World vineyard to make distinctive wines in Martinborough. Hence, Escarpment was born. The vision is deceptively simple yet wholly impressive: to produce tomorrow's definitive New World wine styles. Why change such a recipe for success? To achieve this Larry lives and breathes Escarpment's attitude – "venture to the edge". He continues: "I want to set new directions (especially for Pinot Noir) creating wines of complexity, texture and structure. Our wines are different, full of surprise and perhaps even unconventional. We are proud of our Escarpment Pinot Noir now, but our wines can only get better with ageing vines. The site in Te Muna Valley (translated from the Maori language as 'special place') provides an important part of that edge. Here the Pinot Noir vines are low-yielding, but of outstanding flavour. My challenge as wine maker is to coax all the flavour and character hidden inside the grapes, and create a wine offering immense personality and style. I love the creative elements of wine making – the sense of adventure, the intuitive approach, the thirst to progress and perfect – and the excitement of the final taste in the glass. That thrill never diminishes."

Even though the region is famed for its fruity Pinot Noirs with a savoury edge, leesy and flavoursome Chardonnays and aromatic Pinot Gris, one Escarpment wine which I particularly enjoy is the Pinot Blanc. This fresh, citrus-packed white wine is a great alternative to Chardonnay and a wonderful combination with food. I had the opportunity to visit Margrain, Te Kairanga and Alana Estate. Other vineyards which should not be overlooked, are considered to be 'up-and-coming' and showing good potential are: Schubert, Julicher, Johner Estate (all for their Pinots and Germanic influences), Urlar (for their Pinot Gris and organic methods), Cambridge Road (for their Pinot Noir and Syrah made exclusively by using biodynamic principles) and Nga Waka (for their citrus oil-scented Riesling). Some vineyards have planted small quantites of Viognier too.

Several other towns lie to the west and further north of Martinborough on SH2 (which links Wellington with Hawke's Bay).Foremost among them is Greytown, which has forged ahead with the increase in wine visitors. Those who appreciate unique food producers' stores, farmers' markets, artisan cheeses, excellent restaurants and antique-hunting opportunities will enjoy the authentic village feel of Greytown and the other towns further north. Please do not overlook Masterton, Gladstone and Carterton either, as they offer some local delights and are home to Urlar, Matahiwi, Borthwick, Solstone Estate and

Gladstone Vineyards. Finally, I was delighted to discover, (by way of introduction via David Cox during 2010) a small vineyard on the Kapiti Coast called Ohau Gravels. They are based in Paraparaumu and produce a delicious, yet subtle Sauvignon Blanc, which is decidedly mineral and gooseberry-like. Yes, they produce a Sauvignon Blanc, as do most Kiwi wineries, but it tastes completely different. If you like Sancerre wines from the Loire Valley, then you should definitely try this one. Ohau Gravels also makes small quantities of Pinot Noir and Pinot Gris.

I have also continued to keep in touch with and form new relationships with the talented wine makers and people within Martinborough. For instance, I would regard my times spent in the company of Larry McKenna (Escarpment Vineyard), Lance Redgwell (Cambridge Road), Helen Masters (Ata Rangi), Paul Mason (Martinborough Vineyards), Ant MacKenzie (Dry River), John Kavanagh (Te Kairanga) and Kai Schubert, amongst many others, as some of my most memorable experiences.

As you can see the Wairarapa region has a lot to offer, but do you have the appetite? Wellington is a major transport centre and is the departure point for ferries to the South Island. Safe travels and enjoy the journey across the Cook Straits. We will now say goodbye to the North Island and our next port of call will be Picton in Marlborough and the South Island.

TOP THINGS FOR YOUR "MUST DO" LIST:
Vineyards of Wairarapa and Martinborough
Visit the fabulous restaurants, bars, farmers' markets and coffee shops Wellington and the Waipara region have to offer
Vibrant art and music scene
Te Papa Museum
Kapiti Coast
Castlepoint

Please note: there is a whole host of information in the index at the back of this book.

MARLBOROUGH

MARLBOROUGH

After crossing the Cook Strait on the ferry, you disembark at Picton, gateway to the South Island and to the Marlborough region. For most people, Marlborough is one of the first places which springs to mind when speaking of New Zealand. It was way back in 1987 when I first ever tasted a Kiwi wine and yes, you guessed it correctly – it was a Marlborough Sauvignon Blanc. The region's sunny dry climate is ideal for viticulture, and in the past three decades or more much of the farmland around Blenheim has been transformed into endless rows of vineyards growing grapes. Like me, you are probably curious to find out how it all got started and eager to get stuck in and taste. However, if you have a bit of time, it is worthwhile to spend an hour or two within Picton and explore the quaint harbour, visually-stunning Marlborough Sounds and beyond before dashing off to Blenheim.

The beauty of this wine region is captivating, with a myriad of vines marching across the plains and breathtaking mountains in the distance, framing the horizon from every angle. No wonder Kevin Judd, originally of Cloudy Bay, used that picturesque backdrop of the Richmond Ranges to set the scene, completely encapsulate it and to put it on the now-iconic label. If you want Marlborough on a plate and in your glass – go no further than a Sauvignon Blanc and some delicious fresh seafood. For me this is the pure expression of land and sea and a complete balance of tastes and flavours, which epitomises the region. Marlborough is a region of spectacular natural beauty and remarkable bounty. In the past centuries, Maori hunted moa here and cultivated vast crops of kumara in the year-round sunshine and warm climate. The ocean to the east (yes, there actually is a Cloudy Bay), and the waterways and inlets of the Marlborough Sounds to the north, have always provided all manner of seafood. For instance, Kaikoura, famous for its bountiful crayfish and whale and dolphin-watching, translated means "place of seafood." On the fertile rolling downs, gravel-rich and alluvial soils of the river valleys, early European settlers established the country's pastoral industry and planted extensive orchards. The Marlborough region is noted for its apples, cherries, olives and other stone fruit.

In the 1970s, when the first of the Sauvignon Blanc vines were planted in Marlborough's Wairau River Valley, the farmers of the region had little idea of the tremendous impact those early grapes would have. The rest is history. Today Marlborough is New Zealand's most planted wine region and accounts for around 75 per cent of the country's production. In the span of just a few decades the wines of this small yet geographically diverse region have risen to prominence and attracted the kind of international acclaim more usually afforded the wines of the long-established wine regions of the "Old World." However, it is interesting to note that the family-owned, boutique vineyards can still exist alongside the huge, corporate behemoths. Marlborough produces a wine style to quench anyone's thirst, but can the region cope with our greedy demand?

In 1973, Marlborough's first large-scale, modern vineyard was planted by the Montana company (now re-branded as Brancott Estate) after the region's potential had been spotted by Ivan Yukich, one of the pioneers of the New Zealand wine industry we know today. Montana's was not the first wine to be made from the fruit of Marlborough vines, as the first and original vineyards had been planted a century earlier. In 1873, Scottish farmer David Herd started a wine venture on land known as Auntsfield. This area of land is now within the Southern Valleys sub-region. Over the course of the next century some more pioneering families planted vineyards. During the 1970s when local farmers saw what Montana was doing, committing huge resources to converting traditional sheep and arable farmland to vineyards, they too began to discuss and explore the potential for growing grapes. Throughout this chapter we will delve deeper into the Marlborough region itself and hear a few success stories. Wine quality is inextricably linked to the quality of the environment in which the grapes are grown and there is a high level of awareness about the need to care for the elements that support and sustain the wine industry in Marlborough. After all you cannot make good wine out of bad grapes.

It is no longer just Marlborough Sauvignon Blanc that attracts attention. Chardonnay, Riesling, Pinot Gris, Gewurztraminer, Pinot Noir and also other varietals and wine styles such as sparkling and dessert wines flourishing in Marlborough's suitable climate are now being rewarded with attention and acclaim. This region is a superb area for wine touring, with a wonderful selection of places to stay, ranging from the simple backpackers, hostels and family-owned B & B up to luxury lodges and hotels. Marlborough also has some fine restaurants, bistros and cafés, complementary food producers, butchers, cheesemongers, olive oil producers and farmers' markets and of course winery cellar doors to welcome visitors at every turn. The township of Blenheim is the major centre of the region, but the vineyards extend westwards into the valleys to Renwick and beyond and now cover some of the lower slopes of the Brancott, Omaka and Waihopai Valleys and spill over into the Southern and Awatere Valleys, close to Seddon and Ward to the south. Heading south, the Kaikoura coast is popular with visitors. A fine day out whale watching, either from a helicopter or from a boat, can offer a novel respite from wine tasting, gourmet dining and the many epicurean delights of the region. Hiring a bicycle is another way to get around and at least you won't have to worry too much about drinking and driving by taking this 'more healthy option'.

I think it would be rather churlish of me to talk about Marlborough and not mention the wine that helped put the region and New Zealand onto the world map. Before 1985 Cloudy Bay was a place to go fishing. David Hohnen (of Cape Mentelle) and Kevin Judd newly arrived from Australia soon changed that and ever since that first vintage let us say the rest is history. They created a new wine style, for which not only were they soon to obtain a cult status, but also set the benchmark considered by many wine makers to aspire. Was this luck? Was this being in the right place at the right time? Was it down to spin doctors and boffins in the marketing department? It was some of those things with a good measure of savvy Kiwi innovation thrown in and perfect timing. Quality is probably the most important factor and the secret to success. As Kevin Judd said: "Quality – I know that word seems to have lost its meaning, but it still means a lot to us. We take serious care and attention at every step of the process, in the vineyard and in the winery, and right through to marketing and meeting our visitors." When you stop to think for a moment we have been on this crest of a wave for the past 30 years, it all actually makes perfect sense.

With regards to the last point Cloudy Bay itself has received thousands, if not millions of visitors over the years. It is one of those things you do when you visit Marlborough. You visit the place, you take your snaps, you taste their wines, you breathe in the ambience, and you make your purchases at the cellar door. I have been there and done that many times and I have the t-shirts to prove it. Wine tourism and all the add-ons and other bits and bobs is what Marlborough does extremely well. This is "Brand Marlborough" and Cloudy Bay, amongst others have been at the cutting edge leading the way for many years. No wonder the chaps at LVMH had the vision and business brains to purchase this goldmine back in the 1990s and add it to their growing portfolio of luxury brands. The winery has steadily expanded its range of wines to include "Pelorus", "Te Koko", Chardonnay, Pinot Noir, Riesling and Gewurztraminer. Things have certainly evolved, but a whole tsunami of wine makers have tried to emulate their recipe for success ever since.

Marlborough and Sauvignon Blanc is New Zealand's success story and let us be honest, the wine world would be a different place without Cloudy Bay. For me though, the real stars of the show are the grapes and vineyards themselves. The unsung heroes of the wine world include the viticulturists and farmers who carefully grow the grapes which go towards making truly great wines. These people 'behind the scenes' who deserve much credit include early Marlborough pioneers such as Allan Scott,

Margaret and Ivan Sutherland, Mike Eaton and the Tiller family, amongst others who assisted in this success story by supplying the grapes from their vineyards or by Jane Hunter and Montana who led the way for others to follow. Under Kevin Judd's tutelage, Cloudy Bay has been the breeding ground for some world class wine makers in James Healy, Eveline Fraser and Tim Heath.

Things have now come around full circle. Kevin Judd, the original chief wine maker has left Cloudy Bay and created his own eponymous brand under the "Greywacke" label and is making wine from his own vineyard fruit. I saw him in 2009, during the vintage harvest when he was making his first-release wine using the winery space and facilities over at Dog Point. His wines are very different, with plenty of personality and display exciting flavours. Currently, he is making two types of Sauvignon Blanc and a Pinot Noir. Speaking of Dog Point Vineyard – there is a wonderful story here. Ivan and Margaret Sutherland purchased land and planted grapes in the late 1970s, knowing that their vines would reach optimum age by the time they got around to founding their own label. Ivan planted Pinot Noir alongside the Sauvignon Blanc, gambling on the grape becoming a big thing for Marlborough one day. The gamble paid off. During all this time, grapes from their vineyards were sold under contract to Cloudy Bay and he was the viticulturist. In 1990 James Healy joined as oenologist and they both found that they were a great team. In addition, their wives, Margaret and Wendy worked at Cloudy Bay. In 2002, when Ivan's maturing vines could wait no longer and it was time to leave, they decided to start their own label – Dog Point. The wines are all sourced from their own valley floor and hillside vineyards on the southern side of the Wairau Valley. Ivan and James, "after spending years in corporate board meetings as directors" got back to "hands-on winemaking". Old fashioned values prevail at every step of the process, low cropping, hand-picking, hand-sorting, wild yeast and oak barrel fermenting and ageing. I am going to make a bold statement right now: I can confidently say that the wines from Dog Point Vineyard are my most favourite of all from Marlborough. For me, they are the most quintessential and truly representative of what a Marlborough wine can be – from great vineyards and two immense people at the top of their game. As Ivan Sutherland puts it in his own imitable way: "James and I served our 25 year apprenticeship at Cloudy Bay. Since 2002, we now get our hands dirty, sweep the winery floors and make a bit of wine."

The first time I visited Marlborough was in 2001 and for the six times I have travelled to New Zealand since, I have never failed to return to the region. I made the journey across the Cook Strait by ferry and headed straight for Isabel Estate and Seresin. I used to list their wines whilst I was sommelier at Harvey Nichols and Oxo Tower Restaurant in London. Moreover, I really wanted to see the vineyards and meet the people behind the wines. Robert Wheatcroft of Fields, Morris & Verdin first introduced me to Isabel Estate back in the late 1990's. The vineyards are owned by the Tiller family. At first Michael and Robyn Tiller grew grapes for prominent wine companies, including Cloudy Bay. But in the 1990s, with children growing up and more time to concentrate on the family business, they decided to try their hands at making their own wine. Short of space, the venture had to get going in the tractor shed, but that did not stop 1994 their first vintage being released to great acclaim. For a couple of years or so, Mike was assisted by wine maker Hatsch Kalberer of Fromm. Isabel Estate was born (named after Mike's mother who sadly passed away in 1983). Over the years the winery has grown, without losing any focus and Mike continues to nurture wine making talent. I think of him as being the Arsene Wenger of Marlborough vignerons. When I was there in 2001, Jeff Sinnott was the wine maker, who has since departed and now produces wine down in Otago.

The Isabel Estate range is estate grown, crafted and bottled, giving Michael and Robyn the luxury of having complete control over quality. High-density planting, low yields, organic viticulture practices, minimal irrigation and traditional hand-harvesting reflect the Tiller's fierce respect for the grapes that need only the slightest coaxing to become wines worthy of the label. Their clear vision, values and determination have encouraged their four children – Jane, Luke, Brad and Caitlin, who all work in the winery and to be part of the family business; alongside the extended family of staff. I have always kept in touch and returned in 2003 and 2004, when Ant Moore was wine maker. I remember on that occasion, Mike Tiller picked me up from Picton and asked: "Fancy going out on my yacht?" I thought he was joking, but we actually did. He had just purchased some new sails and rigging and wanted to test them out before going up to Fiji on holiday. To be honest it was slightly surreal, suddenly going around the beautiful Marlborough Sounds on a friend's yacht having just stepped off the ferry half an hour earlier. I just sat back, took it all in and drank some L & P.

One night, we went out with Georgina Wake to a wine bar called Bacchus in Blenheim and had a really fun time. We also enjoyed a delicious lunch together at Highfield Estate. Their restaurant is excellent and the vineyard is set in a picture postcard Tuscan estate, complete with cypress trees, towers and the whole terra cotta thing going on. Their wines are pretty good too and I rather like the "Cuvee Elstree Brut" Sparkling wine. In 2006, when I left Harvey Nichols and went on my six month sabbatical I spent around ten days at Isabel Estate during the vintage harvest. It was really good to spend some time with them, picking grapes, being a cellar hand, doing a bit of this and a bit of that. I had fun and I learned a lot too. I also made some more friends and it was a great experience. Robyn and Mike Tiller always take on interns from around the world for the vintage to work under their wine maker. At the time, Patricia Miranda, originally from Chile, was at Isabel Estate, but she is now at Yealands Estate in the Awatere Valley. During that visit there were a couple of Germans, an American, a Canadian and two from France. I have fond memories of those times, as I was always made very welcome, especially stay in their lodge and enjoy their warm hospitality. But please accept my apologies for my snoring, guys! I visited Clos Henri, Spy Valley and Dog Point with Pattie and Stephanie McIntyre (who now works at

Cloudy Bay after a stint at Wither Hills). Eric Denis, the French sommelier working at Kauri Cliffs joined me on a little jaunt around Blenheim and we visited Huia, Grove Mill, Fromm and Staete Landt together. On my last evening at the vineyard we enjoyed a lovely dinner in the lodge with Pattie, Luke and the rest of the team. Ashley, Inge, Marie and I went shopping in Blenheim to buy the ingredients from the farmers' market. It was Easter weekend, so we wanted to prepare for a feast. Marie cooked the lamb and veggies in a classic French style, Corey barbequed the chops and steaks, and I made a tiramisu and we had plenty of wine to go round. It was super.

During June 2006, Robyn and Mike Tiller came over to London and presented a vertical tasting of ten vintages of their Sauvignon Blanc and Pinot Noir going back to 1996. It was lovely to see them again. By this time, I was at Orrery Restaurant and Isabel Estate always remained a firm favourite on my wine lists. The last time I visited Isabel Estate was in 2009, when I was in the process of touring around the South Island with Nicki and Keri and we popped in to say hello. We have always made the effort to keep in touch with each other and it is truly wonderful to hear their news (normally via email, Facebook and Twitter) that all the family continue to be involved with the business. The vigneronne's baton has been passed onto Jane (the eldest daughter), who continues to preserve the family tradition and wine producing heritage. Sons, Luke and Brad take care of all winery, vineyard and viticultural responsibilities and the youngest of the Tiller clan, Caitlin does the marketing and co-ordinates their tastings, events and cellar door activities.

When internationally acclaimed Kiwi cinematographer Michael Seresin set up his expansive vineyard west of Renwick in the early 1990s, it was on the very edge of the Marlborough wine making zone. Older, more experienced people shook their heads knowingly and muttered about frosts. Since then two things have happened. Under wine maker Brian Bicknell, Seresin Estate has established a reputation as one of Marlborough's premium producers, and newer vineyards have proceeded much further up the Wairau Valley, expanding into terrain that was once considered even more marginal. Since then, three vineyards have been established, thousands of olive trees and hundreds of native trees have been planted, wetlands have been restored and vegetable gardens now provide fresh food for all the staff. What he has created is more than 100 hectares of vineyard planted in Sauvignon Blanc, Chardonnay, Riesling, Pinot Gris, Gewurztraminer and Pinot Noir, and a powerful vision which his team strives to realise. I have met up with Michael on many occasions in London and he used to be a regular at my restaurant and have interviewed him a few times for my blog. When I asked him about his 'ethos' he responded with: "I get an enormous amount of satisfaction from working with others to create something quite different to creating film. Wine and food, amongst other things, to me represent a cultured life. What I aspire to achieve here is to produce the best wine and food that we can. We have embraced the world of organic and biodynamic farming and winemaking." These organic and biodynamic principles are central to Seresin's philosophy. The entire estate uses specifi-cally formulated biodynamic preparations which, along with natural composts and teas, are used to promote healthy soil and healthy plants. In addition, I now have it on good authority via some highly-respected Marlborough wine makers that a small break away group has been created and their aim is to focus on the region's quality, organic and biodynamic farming and viticulture and overall sustainability.

Seresin Estate has always featured near the top of my list of favourite Marlborough vineyards. I first tasted their wines back in 1997 at Oxo Tower and was introduced to the original wine maker Brian Bicknell. You cannot fail to miss the vineyard along Bedford Road past Renwick because the distinctive Seresin "hand" logo is clearly sign-posted and then you see the huge Stonehenge-like rock formation up on the hill. I have visited the vineyard on four occasions and spent a few days there during the 2006 vintage. Not only was that a great personal experience for me, once again to get hands on and learn something more from another person's perspective, but also it was Brian's last year at the helm. He left and went on to establish Mahi – his own vineyard. I met Clive Dougall, who took over as wine maker, and who previously had worked at Pegasus Bay and a chef called Chris Fortune (formerly of Hotel d'Urville in Blenheim and now runs the farmers' market). I never really realised how hard people worked, especially during the vintage harvest, but now I do. You have to get up very early and sometimes work long into the night; it is real hard graft and very physical. At Seresin there was a really good crew with a great ambience, plenty of banter and loud music. I just mucked in and enjoyed myself. Everyone got on with their jobs without any fuss or too many dramas and at the end of the day we sat down together and enjoyed a hearty meal. That was also the first time I ever tasted a whitebait fritter. The simplest of things are always the best!

Stand-out memories for me while spending time at Seresin during 2006 were when Brian took me around Marlborough in his ute. We enjoyed a lovely lunch at Gibbs restaurant on Jackson's Road, which I gather has burnt down after a fire. We visited many vineyards, including "Raupo Creek" – in the Omaka Valley and the site of one of the estate's single vineyard Pinot Noirs, and various other vineyards in Ben Morven, Awatere and Southern Valleys. We popped in to see Simon Waghorn at Astrolabe. Now there is a vineyard to watch. We drove past plenty of land around Seddon being planted with new vines and Yealands and Blind River vineyards, which are both making some interesting wines. Brian has this knack of putting things across very clearly, but it was even better when you are shown exactly from where the wines came and to be able to visualise all the different valleys and terroirs within the region. For instance, he explained how the various sites contribute different characters to the wines. The clay soils provide palate structure – a key element in Seresin wines – and the stonier ground lends them aromatic appeal. Another time was spent on the sorting table with Chris Fortune picking through the Riesling grapes before they went into the press. Brian showed me the process of pigeage (punching down by hand) of the Pinot Noirs. That is seriously hard work! We tasted wines which were going through fermentation and out of barrel. He showed me everything and my eyes were certainly opened to the sheer hard graft and hive of frenetic activity which is a winery. I took some lovely photos too during that trip - check out my roving sommelier photo gallery chapter.

Brian also drove me around to neighbouring Gravitas and introduced me to Pam and Martin Nicholls and their talented wine maker Chris Young. Martin showed me around their vineyards and we enjoyed a sumptuous lunch of local salmon and seafood at the winery. I distinctly remember we spoke about 'experimental varietals' and asked him about Gruner Veltliner, what he thought about it and whether it could work in Marlborough. Unfortunately, I found out later via their UK agent that they had to sell up due to complications. For me, this was a real shame, as I grew very fond of the Gravitas wines and used to list them at Harvey Nichols and Orrery. Brian took me to Riverlands just outside Blenheim, where many wines are produced and we had a quick chinwag with Mike Just. What I soon realised was this huge operation represents a different side of the wine business in complete contrast to our idyllic view of a small family vineyard. I am not saying I was shocked, but it is very helpful to see what actually goes on and have a grip on reality. Marlborough has it all and who do you think produces that £4.99 Kiwi savvy you see on the shelves in supermarkets?

Parts of the Wairau Valley have more than just a little European flavour, which has added a different dimension to the region. Four vineyards, which deserve more than just a mention and have become personal favourites, are Fromm, Staete Landt, Clos Henri and Herzog. These vineyards were established a few years ago by European settlers who came to the region from Switzerland, Holland and France. These families have success-fully developed and fully integrated their own lifestyle, culture and wine making philosophy into Marlborough and their wines have gone on to achieve great acclaim.

I first became familiar with Fromm wines back in the 1990s

when I was building up my wine collection. With Fromm wines you are required to have a certain degree of patience, as they are built to last, but when you open up a bottle they are definitely worth waiting for. A couple of years ago I enjoyed a Chardonnay and a Pinot Noir both from the 1999 vintage and a 1996 Syrah, which I had kept in my cellar and they were still as fresh as a daisy. I decanted the latter wine and served blind it to some friends who came around for dinner. They swore blind that it was an Hermitage from a great Rhone producer. We were amazed by its depth and complexity. The Chardonnay was tense, mineral, restrained and beautifully balanced with delicious, mouth-watering acidity. The Fromm Pinot Noir is much more 'Burgundian' and different to most Kiwi Pinots. Some say that their Pinots are almost 'backward'. The fresh, ripe cherry fruit was there, but the wine had great structure and a lovely savouriness. This quality comes from the age of the vines and they need time. In fact, the first vineyard planted with Pinot Noir grapes in Marlborough was the Clayvin Vineyard. Michael Eaton, the original owner (formerly of TerraVin fame and collaborations with Pyramid Valley) planted it back in 1991 and then later sold it to Fromm. Mike is a very well-respected guy.

Hatsch Kalberer and fellow wine maker William Hoare share a love of music that has stood the test of time, which also reflects their thinking about wine. Most Fromm wines are aged for two or three years before they are released (which is relatively unique in Marlborough) and they are made to be enjoyed for years into the future. Hatsch, who has been making wines in New Zealand for almost three decades, still carries and cares about the values of his native Switzerland where wine, like food, is a very important part of everyday culture. Moreover, cellaring is common and people collect wine, patiently waiting until it has developed maturity, depth and personality. "We are making wines that will evolve over perhaps 10 or 15 years and bring a smile to the face of the buyer who has the foresight to keep it all that time," says Hatsch. "Which is why we prefer to use corks. We don't want the bottle to be completely sealed because age-worthy wines benefit from breathing a little, so natural corks are the most suitable closure for Fromm wines. They feel good too." I would tend to agree with him, as I have always felt good whenever I have consumed a bottle of his wines. As you may be aware, I particularly adore Riesling. The Fromm Rieslings are modelled on the Mosel region in Germany, with its delicate, citrus and floral character, low in alcohol and persistent, mouth-watering acidity. I guarantee that if I manage to convince you with a bottle of their Spaetlese or Auslese you will end up getting hooked on Riesling. Fromm is possibly the only Marlborough vineyard that chooses not to produce any Sauvignon Blanc.

Ruud Maasdam and Dorien Vermaas came to New Zealand from Holland in the late 1990s for a lifestyle change, but they hardly fit the profile of lifestyle wine makers, with its implications of hobbyist dabblings at the weekends. From the start they have taken a meticulous approach – they spent a year and a half on finding suitable land and took the best advice they could from soil scientist Keith Vincent and viticulturist Steve Smith (now a Master of Wine and head of Craggy Range). They have planted a mixture of grape varieties, including Sauvignon Blanc, Riesling, Pinot Gris, Chardonnay, Viognier, Pinot Noir and Syrah. However, the Staete Landt (the original Dutch name for New Zealand) Sauvignon Blanc is not a mainstream commercial style, but shows a blend of New and Old World influences, with a little barrel-fermentation using wild yeast and a portion spending time on its lees for a creamy texture and added complexity. Unlike many Marlborough savvies that are made to be drunk early, theirs start to display particular attractive characters after a year in bottle. On the whole, I really like Staete Landt wines because they have personality, which is more European and they are good with food. They are one of the few producers to make a decent Viognier too. I've met up with them a couple of times and have always enjoyed their company. The last occasion was in 2010 at the wine dinner they hosted at The Providores in London. Staete Landt wines are good with or without food.

I have visited Clos Henri situated further along the State Highway past Renwick into the Wairau Valley on two occasions (2006 and 2009). Not only am I a big fan of their wines, but also I like them because they have a point of difference, which is particularly refreshing. Their wines can perfectly demonstrate that not all Marlborough Sauvignons taste the same. The Clos Henri story goes something like this. Clos Henri vineyard is owned and run by the Henri Bourgeois family whose history and reputation as growers of Sauvignon Blanc and Pinot Noir, in the heart of the Sancerre region of the Loire Valley in France, goes back ten generations. Passionate and well-versed in these two grape varieties, the family set out to discover other places in the world where they might apply their savoire faire and experience. In 2000, Jean-Marie Bourgeois and his family from Chavignol settled in Marlborough. They decided on this location as the soil reflected similarities to their own in Sancerre, where ultra-premium Sauvignon and Pinot Noir could be grown. The first vines were planted in 2001 and Clos Henri was born. The first vintage was 2004. As you can imagine having listed their wines at Orrery Restaurant, I was very keen to visit the vineyard and to see things for myself. I also managed to learn what Greywacke is all about. Essentially, it is the Kiwi version of caillottes (pebbles).

In 2003 the family came across an unused local parish church in the nearby village of Ward in the Awatere Valley. This provided a special link between Marlborough and the Bourgeois' home village of Chavignol, which has a church with which Domaine Henri Bourgeois wines are associated. The church is called the Chapel of Ste Solange (after the local saint and name of Etienne Bourgeois' wife), was restored and became their logo. In addition, the building itself has become their centrepiece to the estate, tasting room and cellar door. I returned to Clos Henri in 2009 during my South Island road trip and it was interesting to see how the wines had developed. The Sauvignon Blancs, which are produced from vineyards on three different soil types – Greywacke (limestone pebbles and stones), Broadridge (mainly iron-rich clay, which provides the palate weight and structure) and Wither (limestone and clay, which provides the fruitiness and complexity) have a wonderful grapefruit character with expressive minerality and elegance. They develop well with bottle age. The Clos Henri Pinot Noirs are bold, fruit-driven, textural yet charming and elegant. The wines definitely have a European style and deserve to be discovered and enjoyed. Subsequently, a new chai and winery building have been added.

The Herzog story is a testament to passion and dedication. Hans and Therese Herzog established a famous and successful winery in Switzerland and then moved it all to Marlborough, New Zealand, driven by the desire to make great wine. In fact the family's vinous heritage stretches back over four centuries. Hans Herzog adored the great wines of Burgundy and Bordeaux in France and began his long search for the suitable piece of land to grow modern French varieties and where they could thrive. In addition, they had already established a Michelin star restaurant with a fabulous reputation for fine cuisine. Then, on a second visit to New Zealand, the lure of an apple orchard on the boundary of the Wairau River proved too great to resist. In 1994 the Herzogs bought the 12 hectare block on Jeffries Road. The microclimate and conditions were perfect and every-thing that Hans had been looking for. They planted Pinot Noir, Cabernet Sauvignon, Cabernet Franc, Merlot, Malbec, Montepulciano, Chardonnay, Pinot Gris and Viognier. Then on Christmas Day 1999, Hans, Therese, their Taggenberg chef and maitre d' bid goodbye to their businesses, families and friends in Switzerland and took off for a new life in Marlborough. My stand out favourite wines from the estate are the Viognier and the Montepulciano. Alongside the winery, Therese has once again created a restaurant of international repute where her warm hospitality and expertise and the skills of her devoted chefs combine to provide a dining experience where the family wines can be enjoyed as the wine maker intended – with great food. I had the good fortune to enjoy a fabulous meal there with Nicki and Keri in 2009. The Herzog restaurant is a must visit whilst in Marlborough and is genuinely a fantastic experience, especially when you feel like treating yourself.

We indulged ourselves on chocolates and truffles and various other delights at Makana Confections. Chocolate can be a real challenge with which to match wines. From time to time I have hosted some pop up tastings and master classes with a couple of great chocolatier friends in London. William Curley makes exquisite chocolates and one of his creations involves passion fruit, mango and dark chocolate. We found to our pleasant surprise that the best wine combination was the Saint Clair "Pioneer Block" Gewurztraminer made by Matt Thomson. The fresh, aromatic, exotic, floral and lychee notes match the tropical fruits in the chocolate perfectly. Try it for yourself. There is some great produce to be found in Marlborough, especially at the local farmers' market (which is now run by Chef Chris Fortune). If you do not fancy a full-blown epicurean feast at Herzog's, then I would recommend the family-run restaurant at Allan Scott's winery on Jackson's Road opposite Cloudy Bay. Then again, you could always try a Renwick pie! Speaking of pies – award-winning wine maker Matt Thomson has his fingers in quite a few. I love the elegant "Hatter's Hill" Pinot Noir made at Delta Vineyard and other exciting wine projects he continues to be involved with.

I took the opportunity to visit a couple of vineyards and people for whom I have much admiration. I re-visited Brian Bicknell, now established since 2007 at his own vineyard called Mahi. His wines have a precise and well-defined line running through them, yet are textural, expressive, flavoursome and elegant. He sources the fruit from good vineyards and knows Marlborough pretty much like the back of his hand. I also stopped in again on Seresin and caught up with Clive Dougall. Seresin have extended their range of wines; all produced organically and biodynamically and exciting times are ahead. They have also increased their Pinot Noir production. The wine which impressed me most was "Chiaroscuro". It is a flavoursome and exotic white blend, inspired by a northern Italian wine called "Vintage Tunina" by Jermann. We tasted the 2007s and 2009s out of barrel and subsequently later out of bottle when they were released. The "Chiaroscuro" is a great food wine. However, it is produced in very limited quantities and you will have to snap it up while stocks last. Clive assured me that because he believes it's of paramount importance that he remains faithful to his wine making ethos, keeping quality at a premium level and to preserve the vineyard's integrity and the fact that every vintage is always unique, the blend may vary from time to time or be tweaked. He also feels that if the wines are not up to scratch, then they won't get released under the Seresin label.

I popped into Framingham and Te Whare Ra. These two vineyards, the former run by Andrew Headley and the latter by Anna and Jason Flowerday are well-known for their Rieslings. In fact, I believe the Riesling vines at Te Whare Ra are the oldest in the region. I really like their wines and I wish more people would drink Riesling. The Kiwi style, especially the Rieslings coming out of Marlborough do tend to be more delicate and Germanic, and display more floral and citrus notes, as opposed to Aussie versions from the Clare Valleys. Time will tell, but I believe New Zealand Rieslings have big potential, especially for their food-friendliness.

In 2009 I returned to Dog Point Vineyard during the vintage and spent some time with the Sutherlands. We got a bit lost in the car en route and I had to call ahead to ask Ivan for directions. We missed the turning off onto Godfrey Road and ended up going around in circles, along Hawkesbury Road past Isabel Estate onto Brookby Road then onto Dog Point Road. We saw the Tuscan-style Highfield Estate, but we kept on missing the turn-off to the vineyard. Ivan said: "Look out for the really big sign and you can't miss it!" We laughed because the sign was tiny, marking a very discreet entrance and no wonder we kept on missing it. By the time we arrived we needed more than just one glass of wine!

Whilst at Orrery Restaurant I used to host regular wine tastings and dinners and on one evening in 2008 it was a great pleasure to host Ivan and James for a tasting. Afterwards we went upstairs for dinner and we had a great time. They returned the hospitality when I returned a year later. We stayed for three nights at the lovely Bell Tower with the vineyards and olive groves all around. It is a 'picture postcard' setting and one of the highlights of my trip to Marlborough in 2009. Ivan took us around the vineyards and showed us the extent of the Brancott Valley, with the legendary "Section 94" block of 'special' Sauvignon on the valley floor. We enjoyed a delicious home-cooked dinner at their residence. I am very grateful to them for their friendship and kindness. I attended the Dog Point wine dinner at The Providores in June 2011 and it was a great opportunity for us to catch up and see each other once again. During the convivial setting, we were treated to some top-notch food and wine and shared some more vinous tales. Since then I have encountered many more Marlborough wines and the people behind them.

Over the years, I have followed quite closely and truly admire the work of Clive Dougall at Seresin Estate, Brian Bicknell at Mahi, the Tiller family at Isabel Estate, the Flowerdays at Te Whare Ra, the Waghorns at Astrolabe, Tamra Washington at Yealands Estate, Patricia Miranda (who left Isabel Estate and is currently working at Yealands), Eveline Fraser at Little Beauty, Tim Heath, Nick Lane and the wine making crew at Cloudy Bay, of course, Kevin Judd at Greywacke and the guys at Dog Point, Mike Eaton, Katy Prescott, William Hoare and also the people at Ara, Brancott Estate, Clos Henri, Forrest Estate, Framingham, Huia, Invivo, Lawson's, Mudhouse, Spy Valley, Staete Landt, Tinpot Hut and Villa Maria amongst countless others. It is always wonderful to see that they continue to push the boundaries in the pursuit of producing great wines. Not only do these Marlborough-grown wines give an honest representation of the wine makers' personality and skill, but also a true reflection of what is actually going on within the vineyard. These are exciting times to be in Marlborough.

I have produced a number of roving sommelier videos, wine reviews and interviews featuring many Marlborough wines and wine makers that can be found in the index section at the back of this book. There are also some mouth-watering recipes with choice wine pairings.

Whilst we're on the subject of food, you must head down the East Coast to Kaikoura. This part of the South Island is well-known for its seafood, especially for its bountiful supply of crayfish. En route you have a couple of options for pit-stops. Kaikoura itself offers some nice simple eateries, but my two jewels in the Marlborough crown are The Store at Kekerengu and "Nin's Bin Crayfish Shack" – both right on the Kaikoura Coast. For me, there is nothing better than sitting on the beach, overlooking the beautiful sea, glass in hand, sipping on some wine and enjoying some delicious fresh seafood.

TOP THINGS FOR YOUR "MUST DO" LIST:
Vineyards and wine trails of the Marlborough region
Visit the fabulous restaurants, bars and coffee shops Blenheim and its environs have to offer
A variety of wonderful places to stay, ranging from homely, family-run B & B's to luxurious and secluded lodges
Marlborough Sounds
Waterfall Bay
Blenheim Farmers' Market
Herzog's Restaurant
Marlborough Wine Festival
Fresh seafood, especially green-lipped mussels and crayfish
Whales and dolphins along the Kaikoura Coast
Yachting and sailing activities

Please note: there is a whole host of information in the index at the back of this book

"If we have a guiding philosophy, it is to work with the natural processes involved in grape growing and wine making, to allow them to proceed to their final result without the need for undue intervention. We admire wines that have poise and finesse, wines that speak more of place than wine maker."
Judy Finn - co-owner and wine maker, Neudorf Vineyards

NELSON

NELSON & THE WILD WEST COAST

Nelson is at the top of the South Island. It also has the highest recorded hours of sunshine, which not only makes Nelson the perfect holiday destination, bit also has a key influence on the region's food, wines and culture. Most Kiwis go there for the sunny beaches, the relaxing lifestyle and the sporting activities of Abel Tasman National Park. The first time I went to Nelson was in 2003. I had just spent quite a bit of time in Marlborough, its rival neighbour and I made the scenic, yet twisty journey through the mountains and valleys to spend a couple of days there before heading on south down the rugged West Coast. I remember when I arrived it was raining. I checked into my hotel, freshened up and went out for a walk to stretch my legs and see what the town had to offer. However, it did not take me long to realise why it was given the local moniker of "Sleepy Hollow".

A region that is renowned for superb art and crafts, and perhaps even with an ambience similar to a 'hippy colony', Nelson is also home to a number of wineries that take advantage of the abundant sunshine and microclimates to grow several grape varietals. Nestled in this mountain-ringed haven is a large coterie of creative talent, including accomplished silver-smiths, glassworkers, potters, sculptors and woodcarvers too. The region's sunny, cloudless skies provide a clarity of light and colour that has attracted many well-known painters over the years. Even though I share the same name as a famous Italian Renaissance artist, sadly I lack the artistic skills to paint, but I do appreciate fine art and photography. Visitors can tour the surrounding countryside, discovering art treasures and the distinctive landscape that often inspires the work. A good time to visit the region is when they are hosting the Nelson Wineart festivities, when many national and international luminaries from within the wine world descend on Nelson and sample the wines. This normally takes place in February and coincides with the "Nelson Aromatics Symposium" and is an ideal opportunity to discover and enjoy the local produce and friendly hospitality.

The history of wine making in the Nelson district goes back to the mid-1840s, when two shiploads of German wine makers arrived with great hopes of success. By 1845, however, most of them had departed mainly to the Barossa Valley in South Australia. For almost the next century, the region's top crops were apples, hops and tobacco. My friend Nicki, who I met in 2007 on a trip to a German vineyard, mentioned that she had some family in Appleby, who were descendants of "the first ships Nelson". This is a mere coincidence, I know, but I got an impression of a genuine sense of pride from her that she could trace her relatives back to those early settlers and pioneers. Family is important. There's more about this and our "2009 World Tour of New Zealand and Road Trip of the South Island" later...

Among the modern day wine makers, the early pioneers were Hermann and Agnes Seifried in 1974 and Tim and Judy Finn in 1978, both in the Upper Moutere and both, most importantly still family-owned. The Seifried winery is now sited with several others on the Waimea Plains around the Appleby Highway. I have had the great pleasure of visiting both vineyards and have been a big fan of their wines for many years. The Seifried family, amongst others are experimenting with Gruner Veltliner. Seifried Estate is the largest and oldest winery in Nelson and a large proportion of their fruit goes out under the "Old Coach Road" label, a brand that is popular in overseas markets. The original site in the Upper Moutere has been taken over by Kahurangi Estate and they now source their grapes from vineyards in the Redwood Valley, Bright-water and the Waimea Plains. Their "sweet Agnes" dessert wine has become a modern Kiwi classic and they also produce a very small amount of Zweigelt (a red grape from Hermann's native Austria).

I believe that even with these two iconic family-owned vineyards at the forefront of the region's and country's wine making heritage, Nelson will always be over-shadowed by its more well-known neighbour Marlborough. Wineries such as Aotea, Brightwater, Greenhough, Kahurangi Estate, Moutere Hills, Te

Mania Estate, Waimea Estates and Woollaston all deserve to be discovered as they make excellent quality wines. Further wineries can be found in and around the Upper Moutere hills and there are several plantings over the winding Takaka Hill in Golden Bay. The Nelson region produces fine aromatic whites, especially Riesling and some good Pinot Gris and Gewurztraminer, and is also gaining a reputation for some excellent Pinot Noirs. We all know that the latter grape variety requires certain conditions to achieve true greatness, but I would encourage anyone sceptical about Kiwi Pinot to taste the "Tom's Block" or "Moutere" Pinot Noir produced at Neudorf or the "Hope Vineyard" from Andrew Greenhough. By the way, allegedly most Kiwis pronounce it "New-dorf", not "Noy-dorf" as in the Germanic way.

One of my favourite Nelson vineyards is Greenhough I first tasted Andrew Greenhough's wines back in the early 1990s. They really impressed me and I have been following them ever since. A star of the region's wine making scene, Andrew has received international acclaim for his Hope Vineyard Pinot Noir. Their style has evolved over the years and could be described as halfway between the earthy, savoury notes of Martinborough and the big, bold and fruitier flavours of Central Otago. In common with several other leading Kiwi Pinot Noir vignerons (such as Clive Paton of Ata Rangi and Tim Finn of Neudorf) Andrew is largely self-taught, though he once worked for Villa Maria as a cellar hand. They cut their teeth and made their mistakes back in the early days, but things came together from about 1997 onwards. He has also planted some Pinot Blanc and Gewurztraminer, which should be interesting.

I vividly remember some wonderful experiences during my initial trip to Nelson a few years ago. These include eating a fabulous meal at Hopgood's restaurant. Kevin Hopgood worked in London at Martin Lam's restaurant "Ransome's Dock" in Battersea. I would definitely suggest you to dine there, as his cooking is top-notch, the hospitality warm and friendly and the extensive wine list is chock-full of amazing Kiwi wines. As well as visiting vineyards in Brightwater and the Upper Moutere, another favourite experience I had whilst in Nelson was going to the Abel Tasman National Park. As Nelson is served by a small airport it is possible to get there via regular domestic flights, but I believe the best way is by car or bike, especially as you travel along the coast and catch a glimpse of the beautiful beaches, bays and sounds. From Blenheim, drive through the early gold mining area of Canvastown and over the Pelorus River. After crossing the Rai and Whangamoa Saddles you reach Nelson city, which stretches ribbon-like around the coast of Tasman Bay from Monaco to Motueka. The main thoroughfares into the city itself are Queen Elizabeth II Drive and Trafalgar Street. Inland from Nelson through the dramatic Richmond and Spooner ranges there is an angler's paradise of rivers and lakes. The coastline is a bountiful haven of shellfish, especially the legendary green lip mussels of Havelock. Do not be surprised by their size, as these local delicacies are big, fat and juicy. The freshly-caught salmon is also tempting and I would recommend you try Mapua Wharf's Nature Smoke Café. As mentioned earlier, coffee has become big in New Zealand. Whilst in Nelson you must visit the charming Pomeroys coffee shop. The smells of the roasting beans and the homely ambience of the shop transported me back to my childhood in Bristol and evocative memories of Cawardines. One could argue that Pomeroys makes the best coffee in the country. I am sure that some of you may disagree.

During 2003 and 2004, I made two extensive road trips around the South Island. For me, the South Island is my favourite island of the two. In fact, I could probably write a separate book about the South Island, especially featuring all my wonderful experiences down the rugged West Coast and I have plenty of anecdotes. When you leave Nelson, following the State Highway 6 south, you pass through some townships and suburbs - Stoke, Richmond, Hope, Brightwater, Spring Grove and Wakefield before heading out into the countryside. The road cuts its way through native forests, national parks and dramatic gorges. The locals call this area "The Big Bush". Incidentally, should you wish to travel back to Blenheim, take a left turn at Kawatiri

Junction and head back through St Arnauds Pass, along the Richmond Ranges and into the Wairau River Valley. Should you carry on the SH6 and pass through the Kahurangi Forest you will eventually reach Murchison and the mighty Buller River Gorge. The sheer velocity and sound of the rapids of the youthful river down below are immense. When you leave the intensity of the Buller Gorge (the location of an epic swing bridge of Indiana Jones proportions) and the Mokihinui Forest (whose river is famed for the legendary whitebait) the SH6 takes you right out onto the coast and the town of Westport. Forget about "Lord of the Rings", when it comes to rugged terrain, this is much more akin to a scene out of "Raiders of the Lost Ark".

The State Highway 6 takes you all the way down the West Coast and from time to time you are right there a mere few feet away from the coastline itself. The whole experience was exhilirating and as mentioned I probably have enough content for another book. Places en route which certainly deserve a mention are: Paparoa National Park and the Pancakes Rocks at Punakaiki, the old historic mining town of Greymouth and the Monteiths brewery. We are not really in wine country here and for many years the staple diet of the hardy inhabitants has been liquid hops. The food is also hearty and rustic. You must try a whitebait fritter - best eaten between two slices of buttered white bread. Whitebait are a highly-prized, local delicacy here and they fry handfuls of the little tiddlers in a pan with some butter and beaten egg and are delicious.

Following the craggy coastline further south the SH6 takes you to places such as Hokitika, where they have their annual "Wild Foods Festival" – a kind of exotic Glastonbury-style food-fest, similar to the one hosted each year in Abergevenny. Hokitika is a very historic town going back to the 1840s and is famed for its excellent quality jade and greenstone. It is a nice place for an overnight stop-over and the nearby Lake Brunner has a luxurious lodge resort too. Hopefully, you will not encounter too many wildlife roaming around in the bush either. There are plenty of tales of the old historic port and quayside and how the ships were battered and wrecked along the beaches.

I enjoyed seeing the glaciers and picturesque lakes at Fox and Franz Josef. The scenery is particularly stunning and if you are a keen photographer, then you should be very happy. On the one side you have the Pacific Ocean, rocks and beaches and on the other the Alps and glaciers. It is a real destination for walkers and fans of Alpine sports and activities. There are stunning vistas of the mountains, Aoraki/Mt Cook and Mt Tasman, the glaciers and the two main lakes of the region: Matheson and Mapourika. If you are more adventurous then you can see this from above up in a helicopter. In the end, my journey down the West Coast took me to Haast, which is a World Heritage site and noted for its bird sanctuary and nature reserve. If you are into native flora and fauna you will be very much at home within these environs. My late Nonna was a keen ornithologist and pretty much knew the difference between all their calls and songs. What she did not know about flowers and plants was not worth knowing either. Even though I do not posses such knowledge or those necessary 'green fingers', I do enjoy those nostalgic moments and reminiscing about such experiences. I still have the pebbles and shells from the beaches which I brought home with me. In fact, at one stage whilst in Haast I got so carried away being in my own little world that I almost missed the coach, which was to take me on to Wanaka. Before I forget, one small tip – whilst on the West Coast look out for "The Lion's Head".

I returned to Nelson in 2009 and this time it was with a couple of friends (Nicki and Keri). One of the highlights of that trip was to be able to visit Tim and Judy Finn at Neudorf. I adore their wines, as I believe they are very expressive and true to their varietal and terroir. Their wines have texture and complexity and have become personal favourites. We enjoyed a lovely tasting at the cellar door, Tim showed me around the winery and vineyards and we ended up on the back veranda sipping on a refreshing Riesling and nibbling on artisan cheeses before heading back. Unfortunately, on travelling through Appleby (Nicki wanted to stop off and visit her grandparents), we accidentally ran over a fox caught in our bright headlights as it dashed across the main road in the gloomy darkness. Needless to say, we didn't take the roadkill back to cook up for our supper, but that "ba-dump-ba-dump" sound will always be with me!

On the following day, we made our return journey back to Christchurch through the spine of the country via the Lindis Pass. At Spring Junction you turn off the SH6 and follow the main road in a south-easterly direction through Maruia and Hamner and their hot springs, via Culverden, Hurunui, Hawarden and Waikari, past Pyramid Valley vineyards and joining the SH1 just north of Waipara. That was quite a road trip and luckily we made it back to Christchurch in time for Keri's shift at the restaurant.

Judy and Tim came over to London during 2010 and I met up with them. They presented many back vintages and current releases of their wines, including the Rieslings, Pinot Gris, Chardonnays and Pinot Noirs at a tasting at Quo Vadis. I also interviewed Judy for my blog. They are such lovely people and the Neudorf wines have stood the test of time. Here is the Neudorf story: "Tim and Judy Finn planted their first vines in the late 1970s, beside the tiny hamlet of Neudorf, established by German settlers in 1842. The vines spill down a gentle north-facing slope overlooking the Moutere Valley. Shallow, sandy loam overlays draining clay subsoil based on the weathered gravels of an ancient river system. The virgin soil is of naturally low fertility and the deep gravely clay retains enough moisture to support the vines through the dry summer months. In the vineyard a combination of high plant density and low yields gives the fruit concentration, texture and palate length, which are hallmarks of Neudorf wines." They are founder members of the New Zealand Sustainable Viticulture Group and "The Family of Twelve".

While the Finns initially earned their reputation for concentrated, minerally Chardonnay, ("Moutere" is perhaps regarded as one of the best in the country), it is their elegant and complex Pinot Noir which has attracted the most attention, especially more recently. It is characterised by a "ripe savoury concentration and linear fine-grained tannins. They are happy to trade sweet fruit for vinosity, texture and complexity and they sincerely believe power should not come at the expense of elegance."

Finally, I would like to encourage anyone to visit the region of Nelson, whichever way you travel there or make your journey or to simply use it as a 'pit stop' before heading south. For to enjoy its tranquil beauty is certainly worth the effort. Personally though, when you visit Nelson you will always discover a special kind of light and energy, which is quite mesmerising. Rest assured, within this quaint paradise you will also encounter some genuinely down-to-earth people, fine wines and top-quality produce. That's guaranteed!

TOP THINGS FOR YOUR "MUST DO" LIST:
VIneyards and wine trails of the Nelson region
Visit the fabulous restaurants, bars, micro-breweries and coffee shops Nelson has to offer
Nelson Wine Art
Abel Tasman Park
Golden Bay and Farewell Spit
Walking, cycling, sailing and watersports

Please note: there is a whole host of information in the index at the back of this book.

"'Many believe this is where the Pinot Noir grail is to be found. Probably the most beautiful wine region in the world."

Jancis Robinson MW - wine communicator

CENTRAL OTAGO AND THE DEEP SOUTH

CENTRAL OTAGO & THE DEEP SOUTH

Allegedly Central Otago has no 'officially designated' borders, yet the inhabitants are adamant that it is neither Otago nor Southland. A high plateau crisscrossed by snow-capped mountain ranges and deep gorges, Central experiences clear, icy winters, when brittle branches glisten with hard frost, and hot, dry summers. Cases of frostbite and sunstroke are not uncommon here. But springtime bursts forth in a pageant of blossom and autumn is a rich palette of burnished leaves. Otago is perhaps the most picturesque region in New Zealand. In addition, I believe that possibly with the exception of dramatic Franschhoek in South Africa and rugged Priorat in Northern Spain, it is by far the most scenic of the world's wine regions. High praise indeed and apart from the obvious draw to the region of copious amounts of fine wine, sheep, outdoor pursuits, adrenalin sports and bungy-jumping, Wanaka and Queenstown have become destinations for travellers from all over the world.

Beside the turquoise waters of the always chilly Clutha River grow scented fields of thyme, and in summer there are orchards of luscious apricots, nectarines and stone fruits. The local rabbits have plenty on which to fill themselves with all of this tasty seasonal produce. Bounded in the north by the St Bathans Range and in the west by the Main Divide, Central Otago encompasses lakes Hawea and Wanaka and spreads south as far as the long dog-leg of Lake Wakatipu and the evocatively-named Shotover River, a popular stretch for jet boating excursions. On the northern shore of Lake Wakatipu lies the vibrant tourist town of Queenstown, servicing the ski resorts of Coronet Peak and the surrounding evocatively-named "The Remark-ables". This area has become the playground for the international jet set, rich and famous, and the not so rich and famous backpackers and students.

In 1891 gold was discovered near Lawrence, and gold fever quickly spread up the Clutha River. Large canvas towns sprang up at Clyde and Alexandra and by 1863 there were 10,000 prospectors, including many Chinese, panning and digging in the area, some of the hardier pushing up into the lakes district and the Southern Alps. The rush for gold had taken off. Cromwell and nearby Bendigo were once thriving gold rush towns. Living conditions were often very primitive and tough. Exposure, freezing waters and unfavourable conditions all claimed their gold-struck victims, as is evidenced by the many Chinese and other foreign names on headstones at the local cemetery. The main street in historic Arrowtown is lined with old wood and stone cottages and sycamore trees that, in memory of its rich past, blaze with a different type of gold every autumn. The Clyde dam near Cromwell and an older hydro dam further south at Roxburgh both harness the power of the mighty Clutha, New Zealand's deepest river.

I have been to the region twice – first in 2003 and then in 2004. The first time was on my road trip down the rugged West Coast on the State Highway 6. My journey took me on from coastal Haast, through the dense, almost tropical and wet forests of the interior via "Gates of Haast" and down towards Wanaka. The SH6 takes you directly between the twin lakes of Hawea on your left and Wanaka on your right. The town itself is very beautiful and if you go there at the right time of year (preferably in autumn) then it is very photogenic. In fact, Wanaka is home to possibly the most photographed vineyard in the country: Rippon Vineyard with the beautiful lake and Mt Aspiring in the background. I am a big fan of their wines, which are farmed using biodynamic practices. Nick Mills spent time cutting his wine teeth at the iconic Domaine de la Romanee-Conti in Burgundy. In 2003, I stopped off at Rippon Vineyard for a tasting before staying overnight in Wanaka. The region may remind you of Northern Italy with its picturesque lakes such as Como, Maggiore or Garda. It has a similar ambience too and you can smell the wafts of money in the clean, fresh air, as it has become a destination for the more affluent traveller. Cardrona is a quaint little place too, especially if you eat and/or stay at the Cardrona Inn. The road takes you on to Cromwell and into the heart of the Central Otago region. You make a turn and follow the road along the Wakatipu Basin with its dramatic views of the Southern Alps and surrounding vineyards of Bannockburn, past "Roaring Meg" and through the Gibbston Valley before reaching Queenstown. It is a wonderful drive through picturesque landscape. But it is even more dramatic when you fly over the mountainous alpine terrain of the South Island by plane and land at the airport at Frankton, which is how I arrived there in 2004. Later in 2009, I would have loved to have had the opportunity to re-visit Central Otago, but alas I did not have the time.

The rush to plant vines in Central Otago over the past recent years has been almost as reminiscent of the gold-rush days. From Queenstown to Wanaka and Tarras, through Gibbston Valley and alongside SH6, around Lowburn, in the hills that surround Bannockburn and Alexandra, on the plains of Bendigo, around Lake Dunstan and now in North Otago's Waitaki Valley, row upon row of new vines can be spotted as investors chance their luck with Pinot Noir, Pinot Gris, Riesling and other varietals. The world of wine has brought with it a new aspect to this region, which is unrivalled in New Zealand for adventure tourism and its spectacularly dramatic scenery. It has fast become the number one destination for thrill-seeking tourists and now also offers an exciting wine scene. Even though I have tasted many wines from the region and continue to do so, year on year new labels are springing up all the time and at a very rapid rate. The older and most original Central Otago vineyards have continued to develop, evolve and improve gracefully and lead the way.

The Central Otago wine story goes something like this. The history of wine goes back to the early days of the European settlement when gold miners arrived here in the 1860s. Among them a couple of Frenchmen grew some grapes and established a little winery in Clyde in 1864. Unfortunately this was not followed up and when they left the region was devoted towards the planting of stone fruit and used for sheep grazing. In 1895 the New Zealand Government brought Australian-based Italian trained viticulturist Romeo Bragato to the country to identify land suitable for grape growing. Central Otago was one of the first places he visited and he enthusiastically endorsed the region as "eminently suitable". Once again the advice was ignored. It was not until the 1970s and early 1980s, a century after those early French settlers, that serious efforts to re-establish wine growing resumed. A handful of modern pioneers planted experimental plots and these bore fruit when the first commercial wine was produced in 1987 by Alan Brady at Gibbston Valley Vineyard. In 1996, Central Otago totalled 11 wineries and at present there are around 90 registered in the region. In a remarkably short space of time Central Otago has earned an international reputation, particularly for its Pinot Noir. The region is now New Zealand's fourth largest and its wines grace dinner tables around the world, regularly winning medals and trophies in all the great wine competitions.

This is the world's most southerly wine region. The gentle valleys have a mellow microclimate similar to that of Tuscany or Burgundy, and their alluvial schist soils and north-facing slopes (the best aspect in the Southern Hemisphere) have began to produce some excellent quality premium wines. Olives are starting to take hold here and the region is now famed for its local delicacy – "Black Gold", a.k.a truffles. This is living life on the edge and the climate is very marginal. Once again the common theme of a distinct lack of traffic abounds here. Those used to being stuck in London's rush-hour traffic on Marylebone Road or in a jam on Hyde Park Corner will be refreshed by the region's relaxed pace. I particularly enjoyed the anecdote which Charlotte Rushworth of New Zealand Winegrowers in London told me: "A couple of years ago I was on a work trip to New Zealand and spent the day in Central Otago visiting wineries in Cromwell and Gibbston. On the way back to the airport the brakes on my hire car failed but I managed to pull over to the side of the road. I stood at the side of the road, a little English girl in work suit and high heels, for nearly 2 hours with not a soul passing on the road. Just as I was giving up hope and preparing to camp under the stars a knight in shining armour came driving down the road and stopped to give me a lift to the airport. My knight was the wine maker at Peregrine and I vowed then and there to make Peregrine my wine of choice whenever I could. As we were driving down the road I asked him if he was going home after a day at work. 'Oh no' he replied. 'I only drive into town once every two weeks!'"

Central Otago has been divided up into six smaller sub-regions, which are now starting to display their own individual terroir nuances and stylistic differences and expression. The sub regions are:

Gibbston—a narrow valley enclosed by mountains where about 250 hectares of vines are planted on sloping, north-facing land on the south bank of the Karawau River. Gibbston is the coolest and highest of the sub-regions with vineyards at between 320 and 420 metres altitude.
Includes the following notable vineyards: Gibbston Valley, Amisfield, Chard Farm, Peregrine, Hawkshead, Mount Edward and Waitiri Creek amongst others.

Wanaka—the smallest of the sub-regions has vineyards planted between the shores of Lake Wanaka and the town of Luggate to the east. At 290 to 320 metres above sea level the vineyards have a similar but slightly warmer climate than those of Gibbston.
Includes the following notable vineyards: Rippon, Maude and Mount Maude.

The Cromwell Basin—contains the largest concentration of vines in an area bounded by the Karawau River, Lake Dunstan and the Pisa Mountain range. It is a warm, early-ripening district dominated by semi-arid, flat to undulating high terraces and moraines (glacial deposits) and gently sloping fans.
Includes the following notable vineyards: Central Otago Wine Company, Karawau Estate, Pisa Range Estate, Quartz Reef, Rockburn, Tarras Vineyards and The Wooing Tree amongst others.

Bannockburn—on the southern banks of the Karawau near

Cromwell is a very warm, dry district where grapes ripen early on sandy, silty loam soils. The altitude here ranges from 220 to 370 metres in an area known by miners as "the Heart of the Dessert". Located along the now-famous Felton Road are a small number of established vineyards with a great reputation. In my opinion, Bannockburn itself could be regarded as the Grand Cru of Central Otago.

Includes the following notable vineyards: Akarua, Bald Hills, Carrick, Felton Road, Mt Difficulty and Olssen's amongst others.

Bendigo—lying east of the Clutha River and Lake Dunstan has both intermediate (220 metres) and higher terraces (330 to 350 metres) planted in grapes. This warm area has semi arid, variable depth, free draining soils at the lower levels with shallower soils higher up.

Includes the following notable vineyards: Misha's Vineyard, Folding Hill and Prophet's Rock amongst others.

The Alexandra Basin—framed by the Clutha and Manuherikia rivers regularly records New Zealand's hottest summer temperatures. Spectacular schist outcrops dominate the arid landscape and a wide diurnal shift (difference between day and night temperatures) moderates the high temperatures.

Includes the following notable vineyards: Black Ridge, Drumsara, Judge Rock, Mitre Rocks, Three Miners and Two Paddocks amongst others.

Of course, perhaps we should add a seventh sub-region to this list of half a dozen? Waitaki Valley in North Otago, near to the border of Southern Canterbury, is the most recent and 'up-and-coming' area and is producing some interesting wines. However, it is still early days, but let us watch this space. Most influential here are Jeff Sinnott (ex-Isabel Estate and Amisfield), Jim Jerram, Dr John Forrest, Michelle Richardson (ex Villa Maria and Peregrine), Pasquale/Kurow Vineyard, Ostler and Waitaki Braids.

Before we proceed on this vinous journey, I would really like to tell you the "Roaring Meg Story".

Back in 2003, whilst I was Head Sommelier at Fifth Floor at Harvey Nichols in London, I had a Kiwi chap in my team by the name of Michael Connolly. At the time Mike was studying for the WSET and I assisted him to hone his sommelier skills by having him work under my wing in the restaurant. He was a good worker, friendly and conscientious with that typical 'can-do' Kiwi attitude and if I remember correctly came from Christchurch. Mike spent a year or so working with me, then went on to a place called "The Engineer" in Primrose Hill. He told me many anecdotes and gave me a few tips on which places to visit and so on when I was in New Zealand. As I was a big fan of New Zealand wines we listed a very extensive selection, but it was always company policy at Harvey Nicks, especially with regards to the wine buying to source interesting and cutting edge labels, as well as having a smattering of the icons and usual suspects. In 2003 and 2004 one of these innovative, up-and-coming Central Otago wineries to enter the stage with a loud voice was Mt Difficulty. They soon attracted some attention and the wines were rewarded with critical acclaim. I used to serve their 'second' wine "Roaring Meg" Pinot Noir by the glass in the restaurant. Anyway, I was rather curious to find out who, what or where this "Roaring Meg" actually was.

Whilst travelling through the valleys of Central Otago, my tour guide declared "and if you look to your right you will see Roaring Meg!" Discovery of gold in the 1860s attracted many young men to Central Otago in search of their fortune – with them followed a number of enterprising young women equally keen to share in the spoils. Meg was one of these ladies. Legend has it she was a high-spirited, fun-loving young thing with an eye for the opportunity, and she set up a "hotel" to "service" the local miners. She quickly became a well known local institution and was nicknamed "Roaring Meg" to reflect her feisty personality. Eventually Meg became so popular that she had a local gorge, river and New Zealand's first hydro electric power station named in her honour.

The power station still feeds the local power grid to this day, and the Roaring Meg vineyards, owned by Mt Difficulty are located just down the road from these landmarks. As well as Pinot Noir, Riesling and Sauvignon Blanc are now produced under the "Roaring Meg" label. I visited the Mt Difficulty vineyards and met Michael Herrick, Matt and Robin Dicey and enjoyed their wines. Most recently, during 2009 I attended an interesting tasting, where several of the estate's Pinot Noirs were put up against some serious red Burgundies and in 2012 at an epic wine dinner hosted at the top-floor restaurant inside "The Gherkin" in London.

During 2003 and 2004, I visited Gibbston Valley, Amisfield (formerly Lake Hayes, where Jeff Sinnott was at the helm), Peregrine, Waitiri Creek (co-incidentally located on Church Lane – only my family will understand the significance of this address), Chard Farm, Quartz Reef, Felton Road, Mt Difficulty and Carrick, amongst others. My stand out memories are probably tasting wines at the cellar door and the boutique cheese-making facility at Gibbston Valley. There, the cellars are rock-hewn and built into the steep hillside and platters of local cheeses and specialities are offered to visitors. Another favourite memory was going to Amisfield and enjoying a lovely tasting and lunch at their bistro. Their "Methode Traditionelle" sparkling wine is good too. For me though the best fizz of the region, perhaps even within the country, is made at Rudi Bauer's Quartz Reef winery. I could have done with a few glasses of that before and after doing the A J Hackett bungy from the bridge across the dramatic Karawau River gorge. More recently, I have tasted and enjoyed some Central Otago wines, which I had put away in my cellar. Right now the 2000 and 2003 Felton Road Pinot Noirs are perfect; as are the 2003 Carrick and Gibbston Valley Reserve. I have also enjoyed the 2004 Cornish Point and Mt Difficulty Pinots, 2005 Bald Hills and a trio of Amisfields from 2005, 2006 and 2007 vintages. In addition, I attended an interesting tasting and master class at New Zealand House in London hosted by Jen Parr (wine maker at Olssen's) where she presented a line up of around 15 of the region's Pinot Noirs. In the final analysis, the older and more established vineyards such as Felton Road, Amisfield and Carrick showed much greater depth and complexity. Time will tell with the potential of the younger wines, yet things are looking good.

I have been an avid fan of Felton Road and Carrick for many years and for me they are the best representation of what Central Otago can produce. Blair Walter at Felton Road is an extremely gifted wine maker and it was great to be able to meet him on a couple of occasions in London for the "Pinot Puzzle" blind tasting and at the annual Clarke Foyster tasting. I video interviewed him for my blog both times and he told me the story of the "Calvert Vineyard". This is a great vineyard, which, should New Zealand classify its wines following the Burgundian model, would definitely deserve "Grand Cru" status. There are three vignerons within the Calvert Vineyard – Felton Road, Craggy Range and Pyramid Valley. I have tried these three expressions and they are all uniquely different, even though they come from the same piece of dirt. In the same way, it would be like tasting three "Chambertin" wines (a Grand Cru vineyard for red Burgundy, which produces great Pinot Noir) from different domaines. It was wonderful to meet up with Steve Green from Carrick again too. Many videos and blog articles are featured in the index section at the back of this book.

Another vineyard which has become a personal favourite is "The Wooing Tree". It is a family-owned, single vineyard estate situated next to the town of Cromwell. A local landmark, the Wooing Tree sits prominently in the middle of the vineyard and has long been a popular place for locals to 'woo' their lovers. Steve and Jane Farquharson and a couple of others were working in the UK as IT professionals, but yearning to return home to New Zealand for a lifestyle change and to work on the land. They decided to join forces and look for a site in Central Otago to produce the very best wine possible. Steve, having completed his degree in wine making and oenology at Plumpton College in Sussex, found a nice plot of land in 2002. The development of the Wooing Tree vineyard began. Specialising in Pinot Noir, their aim is to produce rich and intense fruit from low-yielding vines. They also make a "Blanc de Noirs" wine called "Blondie", a Chardonnay and a pink wine and have gone on to win many accolades and awards. For further details, please check out my blog articles and roving sommelier videos in the index section.

Queenstown is an ideal location to use as a base for various excursions around the region. The city itself is a great destination with much to offer, especially with its sophisticated dining scene and exclusive hotels and resorts. The best restaurant has to be Saffron located in Arrowtown. Chef Peter Gawron is a New Zealand culinary legend. You must go there as his food is exceptional and the menu always features locally-sourced ingredients and the wine list packed full of Kiwi gems. I stayed right on the lake and the views of The Remarkables are breath-taking. I would get up early and go for long walks. Unfortunately the old steam ship TSS Earnslaw was out of action. The more adventurous of you may wish to take the Skyline Gondola and brave the rapids of the Shotover and Karawau Rivers. My real highlight was a trip down to Te Anau and Milford in Fjordland. Here you could be in Scandinavia or parts of Scotland. Before going down through the one track tunnel we stopped off by the side of the road. The coach driver advised us to get out and fill up our bottles with the pure spring water that the mountain stream gushed. I sampled it and it was absolutely delicious - so fresh and clean and possibly the best water I have ever tasted. The lakes at Te Anau and Manapouri are stunning with the Kepler and Murchison mountain ranges in the background. The narrow and steep tunnel goes right through the heart of the mountains and comes out at Deep Cove. Here you can tour around the magnificent Doubtful Sound. As you cruise down this superb fjord, various features become apparent: hanging valleys – the remnants of tributary glaciers – are one of the most obvious (I knew my A level Geography would come in handy one day), and numerous waterfalls tumble down the sheer rock faces, with rainbows often adding to the enchantment of the scenery. If you are lucky you may be able to spot some dolphins frolicking and penguins waddling too.

All this talk is now making me hungry again. Onwards to Invercargill, which is right at the foot of the South Island. The only reason why I wanted to visit this quaint Scottish-inspired town in the middle of nowhere was because of my love of oysters. This is the home of legendary Bluff oysters. They are big, fat and juicy and I adore them. With just a squeeze of lemon and a twist of pepper – I am a very happy bunny thank you very much. Picture that scene in the movie "Cool Hand Luke" when Paul Newman sat down and ate around 50 hard boiled eggs. Well it was a similar situation with me in Invercargill when I had my fill of Bluff oysters, waddled back to the coach and chillaxed with a big satisfied smile on my face and counted sheep on the return journey to Queenstown. From there I travelled over to Dunedin for an overnight stop over. I remember the trip up the east coast by train via Oamaru and Timaru to Christchurch was quite scenic. In these parts some excellent cheeses are produced at the Whitestone Dairies. Given the opportunity, I really recommend you visit them. The wines of the Waitaki Valley are well-worth discovering too.

My second journey from Queenstown to Christchurch was even more eventful and dramatic. You are in for a treat when you travel right the way up through the alpine spine of the South Island. Your journey by road will take you through the heart of Central Otago and directly into Canterbury and to its capital Christchurch. At Cromwell, the road takes you in a northerly direction towards Tarras on the State Highway 8. This main road runs parallel to the SH6 which makes its way on the other side of Lake Dunstan. Following the SH8 will take you up through the Lewis Pass to Omarama where the road forks. If you take the SH83 this will lead you east over to the coast and you will come out at Oamaru. However, if you carry on along the SH8 travelling north you will eventually reach Twizel. The ski fields and Lake Ohau will be on your left, but straight ahead you will see the majestic snow-capped peaks of Aoraki/Mt Cook and Mt Tasman. Turn off the road at the base of the mountains at the southern edge of Lake Pukaki and the route will take you right up to Mt Cook itself. Perched magnificently high up in the mountain ranges is the Hermitage luxury resort and hotel. It is quite surreal as you feel that you are in Switzerland. By all means stay there if you wish, but I just got out, stretched my legs and had a coffee break. You then make your way back down the lake and onto the SH8. Mike Connolly advised me another suitable place to get out and take a break. Lake Tekapo is very scenic and there is the Church of the Good Shepherd with its iconic statue of the sheep dog. This area makes for a nice little pit stop. The road will eventually take you on to Timaru, but on this occasion I travelled up through Fairlie and Geraldine, which are in the area known as the MacKenzie Country. Rest assured you will see a lot of sheep here and you are now entering Canterbury. In total this journey from Queenstown to Christchurch should take around 8 or 9 hours, but it is well worth it as you will experience some beautiful countryside. Do not forget the last time I was in this region, the England rugby team were flying high with back to back victories at Twickenham against South Africa, Australia and the All Blacks. They then went on to win an historic victory against the All Blacks on their own turf in "The Cake Tin" and we all know what happened versus the Aussies at the Rugby World Cup Final in Sydney in 2003! Whilst travelling around the country in 2004 I wore my rugby jersey with pride. I hope that when I next return to Central Otago, I will be able to discover all the many new things that have taken place since. The characterful wines and the dramatic landscape of the region certainly capture your attention. Otago is an exciting place to be.

Over the years, I have followed quite closely and truly admire the work of Blair Walter and the Greening family at Felton Road, the Diceys at Mt Difficulty, Steve Green and his team at Carrick, Rudi Bauer and his team at Quartz Reef, Michelle Richardson, Jeff Sinnot, Jim Jerram, the guys at Akarua, Amisfield, Bald Hills, Chard Farm, Gibbston Valley, Judge Rock, Misha's Vineyard, Ostler, Pasquale, Peregrine, Prophet's Rock, Tim Kerruish of Folding Hill Vineyard, Hayden Johnston at Tarras Vineyards and Nick and Jo Mills at Rippon Vineyard, amongst others.

I am delighted to see that they continue in their shared pursuit of excellence and desire to make top-quality wines. For me, not only do these Otago-grown wines give an honest representation of the wine makers' personality and skill, but also a true reflection of their own unique terroir. These are exciting times to be in Central Otago, especially since new vineyards seem to be springing up each year, yet the more established ones have gone on to become icons. The small handful of vineyards on the expressive limestone soils of the Waitaki Valley are starting to show real potential too, especially for Riesling, Chardonnay and Pinot Noir.

I have produced a number of roving sommelier videos, wine reviews and interviews featuring many Otago wines and wine producers that can be found in the index section at the back. There are some delicious recipes with wine pairings. Enjoy!

TOP THINGS FOR YOUR "MUST DO" LIST:
Vineyards and wine trails of the Central Otago region
Visit the fabulous restaurants Queenstown, Arrowtown and and its environs have to offer
A variety of wonderful places to stay, ranging from homely, family-run B & B's to luxurious and secluded lodges
Fox and Franz Josef Glaciers and the Southern Alps
Walking, winter sports, skiing and snowboarding activities
Helicopter rides that include panoramic views
Pancake Rocks at Punakaiki
Lakes: especially Matheson, Manapouri, Te Anau, Hawea and Wanaka
Wild West Foods Festival in Hokitika
Fjordland National Park, Milford and Doubtful Sounds
Queenstown, Lake Wakatipu and The Remarkables
AJ Hackett Bungy, Shotover Jet and Karawau River Gorge
Whitestone Dairies in Oamaru

Please note: there is a whole host of information in the index at the back of this book.

CANTERBURY

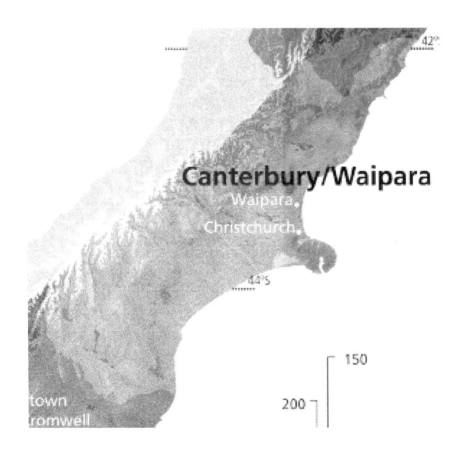

CANTERBURY

Very poignantly we are going to finish our 'road trip' around New Zealand in my favourite region and my favourite city – Canterbury and Christchurch. For me, the best thing about travelling to a foreign country is giving you a reason to return by not trying to cram everything all in one go. At least when you go back you will have a genuine opportunity to visit some new places, meet some more new people and enjoy some new experiences. I have visited Christchurch now four times and on each occasion the experience has just got better and better. In fact, in 2009 I seriously considering living there. Not only is it a beautiful city, well-situated half-way down the East Coast between Blenheim and Dunedin and within easy distance of the Southern Alps, but also I have connections with friends and family there. The wines from the Waipara region, just an hour's drive north of the city, are possibly the most underrated in the whole of New Zealand. Waipara contains a small handful of wineries, some of which, especially with regards to Riesling and Pinot Noir, are the best the country can offer. The region includes some of my all-time favourite Kiwi wines. However, on a personal note what makes this region and city my favourite of all are its people. Christchurch always manages to evoke fond memories of when I lived in Oxford, and that of course means the time when I met 'my first real best friend', David James.

As I explained in the previous chapter, I have arrived at Canterbury via various routes and directions, including from the south through the Mackenzie Country, Geraldine, Timaru and Ashburton. I have flown into and out of the international airport at Christchurch, which is useful should you wish to remain focused on travelling around the South Island and not traipse elsewhere. My favourite way of getting to the city is along the coastal route from Blenheim (a journey I made in 2006 after finishing vintage experience). Driving along the rugged, untamed Kaikoura Coast towards Canterbury, the traveller is struck by the huge contrast between these two areas. The rocky coastline seems remote, with no sign of humanity for miles except perhaps a lonely caravan selling fresh crayfish or an early-morning fisher heading out in a small boat to cast a line or set craypots. If you are lucky you may see whales blowing, or perhaps a school of dolphins. Or rounding a headland you might spot a family of seals basking on the rocks below. The Seaward Kaikoura range, at the northern end of the mighty Southern Alps, towers above the village of Kaikoura like a colossus, especially dramatic in its snowy white winter coat.

After leaving the coast and over the hills to the Canterbury Plains, the whole scene changes. Around Cheviot, Rangiora and Amberley expanses of pastureland are watched by stately country houses, while seemingly endless straight roads vanish into the distance. Here there are several opportunities for a pit stop. I would especially recommend the NorWester Café and the Brew Moon Café and the locality has some wonderful farmers' markets, lodges and places to stay too. Among the tussock-covered foothills of the Alps are some of New Zealand's great sheep stations, the largest being Molesworth, whose 1800 square kilometres sprawl over the boundary between North Canterbury and Nelson-Marlborough. On its southern perimeter, along the Lewis Pass route to Nelson, is Hamner Springs, a nineteenth-century spa town on the edge of a magnificent deciduous forest. We travelled through these parts on our 2009 road trip from Nelson back to Christchurch. At Waikari and Hawarden there are a couple of boutique wineries that are definitely 'must-visits'. Bell Hill (Marcel Giesen) and Pyramid Valley (Mike and Claudia Weersing) have achieved a mini cult status and produce a small, yet excellent selection of wines. Both vineyards are especially highly regarded for their Pinot Noirs and I am rather fond of the Bell Hill Chardonnay and Pyramid Valley Pinot Blanc too. Please note that you will need to make an appointment should you wish to visit them. It is probably not advisable to 'rock up' at the vineyard like I did at Dry River in Martinborough in 2002!

Canterbury's English charm is nowhere more evident than in the city of Christchurch (a.k.a "The Garden City"). The Avon

River flows through its centre, and in its northern reaches local teams practise throughout the summer for the annual secondary schools boat race. Along the tree-lined Oxford Terrace you will see Antigua Boatsheds, built in 1882 and the sole survivor of half a dozen or more similar boatsheds which once stood on the riverbank. Being a native of Bristol, in South-West England, I was rather charmed by the fact that the city's river is also called Avon. As mentioned, the general ambience is more like Oxford and I soon reminisced of punting on the river. Strolling through Hagley Park, in the centre of the city, you may pass a group of schoolboys from Christ's College in traditional blazers and boaters, giving the illusion that these are the playing fields of Eton and Harrow. The park is attractive and I definitely would suggest visiting the Botanical Gardens nearby. This neighbourhood is quite a salubrious part of Christchurch and contains the rather swanky boutique George Hotel and its iconic fine-dining restaurant.

The area of central Christchurch is truly impressive with its historic buildings and Gothic architecture along Oxford Terrace, Worcester Boulevard and Hereford Street culminating at Cathedral Square, which is the location of the now-ruined cathedral. It is worthwhile to spend a little bit of time around here and within the arts centre itself, which boasts a wonderful selection of bars, restaurants and cafés. Annie's Wine Bar is one of my favourites, which has an amazing wine selection and serves simple homely fare. Christchurch also has some great coffee shops, as in New Zealand, especially with cosmopolitan cities such as Auckland and Wellington they do take coffee seriously. Along Oxford Terrace and Worcester Boulevard you will find a whole host of places to frequent. My favourites include Caffe Roma, Le Bon Bolli and Cooking on Gas. It is also a good idea to take the tram around the centre of Christchurch to see the various tourist sights and attractions.

With regards to dining experiences, I have some very fond memories of "Saggio di Vino" and Celia Hay's eponymous restaurant both located on Victoria Street. In 2009 I celebrated my birthday at the award-winning Saggio di Vino with some close friends and family and we were well looked after by Lisa Scholz and her partner Yommi. Their food was probably the best I had ever experienced in the city and they have a spectacular wine list which has won many accolades. Unfortunately, I heard their delicatessen, bakery, cheese room and restaurant operation called "Petrini" (named after Carlo Petrini of the Slow Food movement) in the suburb of Ferrymead was closed down. That passionate couple deserve all the success they can get, after emigrating to New Zealand from their native Germany many years ago and setting up their home and business in Christchurch.

Celia Hay not only owns and runs her restaurant business, but also the New Zealand School of Food and Wine. There she and her team teach and mentor students who go on to earn their stripes and qualifications within the hospitality industry. The restaurant is particularly noted for its succulent and excellent quality lamb, which is sourced from her family farm. She also runs a successful restaurant and food store in Duvauchelle on the Banks Peninsula. I sincerely hope that all is well with them and that the earthquakes did not cause too much devastation to their lives and businesses.

Nearby, a couple of blocks away there is a great cheesemongers owned and run by Martin and Sarah Aspinwall. The couple both set up their business in Christchurch after emigrating from England a few years ago. Martin cut his teeth working at Neal's Yard Dairy in London and has created a wonderful cheese-mongers packed full of his knowledge, experience and artisan cheeses. I have it on good authority (via their Facebook fan page) that they have now re-located (since the earthquakes). Their shop also sells local produce, including artisan breads, chutneys, jams, pickles and other tasty morsels. Speaking of which, I also visited a couple of breweries. Canterbury Breweries are located on St Asaph's Street and they host regular tours and tastings for visitors. The microbrewery called "Three Boys Brewery" in Woolston impressed me too. Their artisan style beers, including original heritage recipes for "Porter" and "India Pale" are very good. We enjoyed lovely meals at Restaurant Schwass run by Johnny Schwass and a place called "The Bicycle Thief", which serves authentic wood-oven pizzas. There are plenty of bars to choose from around the city centre and the little network of arcades and streets known as "SOL" - along Manchester Street, Durham Street, Colombo Street, Lichfield Street, Tuam Street, Madras Street, Cashel Street and High Street. One particularly memorable experience was at "Le Plonk" where the bar tender gave me a 'blind tasting' of a wine to test my taste buds. It was the Wooing Tree "Blondie" from Central Otago. Unfortunately, I am led to believe that most of these places in the centre of Christchurch suffered much upheaval and bore the brunt of much devastation during the earthquakes. I am sure whenever you visit the city now, things will have changed dramatically.

I enjoyed travelling through the suburbs, including Moncks Bay, Clifton and Richmond Hill out to the coast. Two of my closest friends, Sarah and Toby, lived in Sumner and worked at Christchurch Hospital. The views from the Port Hills here up the coast and of New Brighton with its beaches and Pegasus Bay, especially from the gondola are spectacular. We travelled down to Lyttelton Harbour and Governors Bay. The windy roads along the coast, bays and inlets provide excellent terrain for avid cyclists and mountain bike enthusiasts too.

The first four ships docked at Lyttelton Harbour in 1850, and by 1853 over 3500 carefully vetted migrants had arrived. By 1855 Christchurch itself was prospering. The great explorer Robert Scott used Christchurch as the port base from which to make his historic voyage to the Antarctic. There a statue of him in the centre of the city – as there are of Queen Victoria and Captain Cook too. When he circumnavigated New Zealand, Captain Cook mapped Banks Peninsula as an island, an understandable mistake to make as the spit of land connecting the peninsula to the mainland is very low-lying. This bridge of land is bordered on the south side by Lake Ellesmere, a broad expanse of water, rich in eels and flounders. Banks Peninsula is a distinctive knobbly piece of land jutting just to the south of Christchurch and is the South Island's most notable volcanic area. The two massive craters which form Banks Peninsula now shelter two harbour areas – Lyttelton (the port of Christchurch) and Akaroa, almost a French colony. Captain Jean Langlois tried to establish French sovereignty by colonising the peninsula. Even though they were prevented by the English settlers and Maori tribes from gaining any more land, the French legacy still lingers on in the charming port of Akaroa. It is very quaint and for a brief moment you may think you were actually in St Malo. There are only a handful of French-speakers here today but the French street names remain, as do the patisseries and cafés. Akaroa makes for a great day trip or, even better, a weekend excursion. The salmon is a particular speciality of the region and most of the restaurants serve up a traditional plate of fish and chips too. Nearby in Barrys Bay, the cheese farm, the French Farm Winery and Celia Hay's Restaurant and Foodstore in Duvauchelle are worthwhile stop offs should you feel peckish. Whilst you're in Christchurch, two more stalwart must-visits are: Hemingway's Wine Shop has an amazing selection of fine wines and hosts regular tastings and the microbrewery at Brew Moon Café north of the city in Amberley. Both places are definitely worth checking out and the latter serves up a decent flat white and slab of carrot cake too.

Let us now turn our attention to wine and the region of Waipara. Less than an hour's drive north of Christchurch, the wine region of Waipara first captured attention when plantings in the early 1980s yielded Amberley Riesling.. The region has always been known for this grape variety and a handful of producers, such as Pegasus Bay, Muddy Water, Daniel Schuster and Black Estate make notable examples. Original plantings of grapes can also be found at the Glenmark and St Helena vineyards. At Glenmark, John McCaskey, whose family has farmed the western side of the Waipara Valley since 1936, was truly a man 20 years ahead of his time. Inspired by a vineyard trip while touring around Australia, he first planted some grapes on the property in 1965. They proved to be successful with a few wins at some prestigious wine shows during the 1980s. St Helena is the oldest commercial winery in Canterbury and was where Daniel Schuster made the wine before creating his own eponymous label during the 1980s. St Helena, even though like other local producers such as Giesen have focused more on Marlborough still produce their wines at the Belfast winery.

For me the two names that helped Waipara to gain any real prominence and reputation were Daniel Schuster and the Donaldson family. They proved to be a key influence on developing the region's wines, not only for Riesling, but also for Pinot Noir. Prague-born Schuster is perhaps the only Kiwi wine maker who can claim to be at least as known overseas as in his adopted home country. He has worked as consultant to such prestigious wineries as Stag's Leap (in California) and to the Tuscan Antinori family. He is also a pioneer of Canterbury winemaking, having been instrumental in the establishment of St Helena in 1981. It was while at St Helena that he produced a 1982 Pinot Noir that provided an early benchmark for the variety in New Zealand. He stands proudly at the top of the tree with such other luminaries as Clive Paton, Larry McKenna and Tim Finn as being regarded as the patriarch of Kiwi Pinot Noir. His own winery, established in 1986, produces Pinot Noir, Chardonnay and Riesling off the Omihi Hills and Hull family vineyards in Waipara and the Petrie Vineyard beside the Raikaia River in mid-Canterbury. Having been a big fan of him and his wines for many years, I was very keen to meet him and visit his vineyards. In 2009 I drove up with Nicki to meet him. One thing he is not short of is charisma and he could probably talk the hind legs off a donkey with all his wonderful anecdotes. My favourite quote from the great man is: "When I first came here in the 1970's the annual consumption of New Zealand wine was three litres per person. The Italians would spill more than that on their tablecloths!" It was a real pleasure to meet up with him at the wine tasting and lunch at The Bleeding Heart in London later on during 2009. But it was very disappointing to hear shortly afterwards that he had gone into administration. His wines may still be available and let us see what happens in the future. But for now, allegedly you might be able to catch him making wines on Waiheke Island or elsewhere. I am sure he will bounce back after this setback.

The Donaldson family at Pegasus Bay have been seriously involved in wine since the early 1970s and were pioneers of the local grape growing and wine making. Associate Professor and Consultant Neurologist, Ivan Donaldson is a wine writer and wine judge. He also oversees viticulture and wine styles. Ivan's wife Christine is still involved in the business though directs most of her energy into maintaining the winery's extensive grounds. She is also a passionate opera lover and has been heavily involved with Canterbury's Opera scene for many years. She has organised a number of operatic concerts at the winery's natural amphitheatre. A reserve range of wines, which are produced only selected vintages have been dedicated to Christine's passion for opera: "Bel Canto" (Riesling), "Aria" (Late-picked Riesling), "Virtuoso" (Chardonnay), "Prima Donna" (Pinot Noir), "Maestro" (Merlot/Malbec), "Finale" (Noble Chardonnay) and "Encore" (Noble Riesling). They produce benchmark Rieslings and Pinot Noirs and their wines are great with food. In fact, I think their wines are best enjoyed with food. I have met the family several times and visited the vineyard on a couple of occasions and have attended two Pegasus Bay wine dinners at The Providores and The Modern Pantry in London.

For me though, the real highlight at Pegasus Bay is the winery restaurant and tasting room. Their intention is to give the diner a total food and wine experience. The menu is created around the wine selection, each dish being matched with a suggested wine. This and the centrepiece fireplace, the warm and friendly hospitality and the two chandeliers made out of recycled wine bottles are great reasons to visit the family-run restaurant. It is a real 'hands-on' family business: son Matt and his wife Lynette are the wine makers, Ed and his partner Belinda run the restaurant and take care of marketing, whilst youngest son Paul, who has an MBA, manages the business.

Three other Waipara vineyards I have followed for many

years are Mountford, Muddy Water and Waipara West. Nicki and I drove to meet Kathryn Ryan and Taiwan-born wine maker C P Lin at Mountford Estate. I remember a similar sensation came over me to the feeling I had in 2001 when I made my 'pilgrimage' to the great vineyards in Martinborough. C P Lin, who is actually blind, showed us around the vineyards, including the steep "Gradient" planted with Pinot Noir and the small winery buildings. After that small tour we had built up a sufficient appetite to sit down with the winery crew and our host Kathryn to a delicious lunch. Someone told me that like me C P was rather passionate about Alsatian wines, so I purchased a bottle at Hemingway's in Christchurch. We opened it up and during lunch for a bit of fun I wanted to test his palate. He literally did a blind tasting and he got the wine spot on – a Pinot Gris "Cuvee Laurence" from Domaine Weinbach. The actual vintage now escapes me, but I was suitably impressed. Before we departed, Kathryn generously gave us a huge bag of whitebait to take back to Christchurch with us. On our return to Nicki's parents' house in Merrivale, we cooked up some more fritters for supper. Scrumptious!

After our visit to Mountford, we still had enough time and sufficient petrol in the tank to make the short journey down the road to Muddy Water Vineyards. For those who are not aware, Muddy Water is the English translation of Waipara. Over the years, I have really begun to like their wines and we made a quick tasting and met Belinda Gould. I have much admiration for her and she is a very talented and highly-regarded wine maker. She cut her wine teeth in California working for the legendary Josh Jensen at Calera, who is well-known for his Pinot Noirs. Here in Waipara, Belinda crafts flavoursome and elegant wines. Not only has she continued to specialise in Riesling (one of my personal favourites is the Muddy Water "James Hardwicke") and their various Pinot Noirs, for which the region is noted, but also makes Syrah and Pinotage. Muddy Water has now been acquired by fellow Waipara winery Greystone. I am glad to see that they have continued the good reputation and success for which the vineyard has become known. Quantities of both Mountford Estate and Muddy Water wines are relatively small, but they are well worth looking out for.

Finally, I wholeheartedly recommend that you search out wines produced at the small, family-owned vineyard Waipara West. Located on the Ram Paddock Road in Amberley, the Tutton family have been producing small quantities of citrus oil-scented Riesling, silky and elegant Pinot Noir, packed with cherry fruit and a bold and seductive Bordeaux blend at the estate. I first tasted their wines during my time at Fifth Floor at Harvey Nichols, where we listed them, between 2003-2006. I seriously think that Waipara West wines represent great value for money and are well worth discovering. Paul Tutton also owns Waterloo Wines (a small, independent wine merchant) close to the South Bank in London. I see him around from time to time and it is always good to catch up and have a chinwag.

I am very much looking forward to returning to the Canterbury region once again, especially seeing as I am a big "Crusaders" fan. So, for the time being dear readers, this is where our road trip around New Zealand comes to an end and your friendly tour guide is bidding you a fond farewell. For me, it has been an absolute pleasure. All the best and I hope you enjoy the rest of your journey. Arohanui.

In the meantime, you can follow our tweets and updates on Twitter @rovingsommelier and on our Facebook page.

TOP THINGS FOR YOUR "MUST DO" LIST:

Vineyards and wine trails of the Canterbury and Waipara wine regions

Visit the fabulous restaurants, bars, coffee shops and farmers' markets Christchurch and its environs have to offer

A variety of wonderful places to stay, ranging from homely, family-run B & B's to luxurious and secluded lodges

Waipara Valley Wine and Food Festival

Summer of Riesling

Botanical Gardens in Christchurch

Akaroa and Banks Peninsula

Aoraki/Mt Cook

Lake Tekapo

Hamner Springs

Arthur's Pass

Lewis Pass

Lindis Pass

Please note: there is a whole host of information in the index at the back of this book.

The next chapter may make you giggle, but hey, life does not have to be so serious? You never know you might find these few words and phrases useful on your travels. Kiwi slang defines us as Kiwis, warts and all. We are inveterate travellers, we export as well as import words and phrases. In this informal area, nobody can claim absolute authority. The main thing is to enjoy our distinctive language, slang, which defines us as surely as our accent. If you want an example, try 'togs' on any visitor to these shores. Be a happy Kiwi camper!

GLOSSARY OF KIWI SLANG

A few words about language and vernacular

I have shared with you a few anecdotes about food and wine and some useful tips about grape varieties. You are armed with some suggestions of places to visit and a few choice words of wisdom, with the benefit of some experience before you depart on your road trip. In addition, there is a whole wealth of information stored in the back of this book within the index sections.

However, you may be aware that there is still one important topic that needs to be covered. This is the one of language or as they say "getting down with the lingo." You may be familiar with a scenario – you walk down the street or enter a room and you encounter people having a conversation. They are talking with antipodean accents which you can't quite pinpoint. You ask them, "Which part of Australia are you from?" They turn around and look at you with fierce daggers and say in a distinctly unimpressed tone, "Actually we are from New Zealand!" I have made that faux pas on numerous occasions, much to my embarrassment. How does one tell the two accents apart? Apparently, you ask them to say "fish and chips". The ones who pronounce it "fush and chups" are normally the Kiwis. So there you have it…

I thought I would also give you a few idioms and words of Kiwi 'slang', which you may or may not find useful. Essentially, it is a selection of words and phrases, which I have collected over the years, either via family, friends and colleagues or overheard conversations. The slang or colloquialisms that are irrefutably Kiwi are a mix and muddle of Maori and English, the likes of "electric puha" and "up the boohai".

I will also divulge another little secret about me. I am obsessed with words, language and from where they are derived. I especially adore double-entendres. Our more formal educators share with the French the dread of the classical language and grammar being polluted by mongrel imports. The opposite end of the spectrum applies when slang, the cutting edge of language developing at the street and school and social level, is disappearing before it ever makes the formal records. Of course, nowadays, a whole new culture and genre in slang has developed via the internet and social media e.g. Google +, You Tube, Twitter and Facebook and texting in general. Nowadays, it is normally accompanied by a hashtag too. However, slang is rarely the exclusive property of a single nation state; even less so in these mobile times. Slang does not respect national borders. Sometimes slang can be used positively or negatively or basically quite offensively. Slang is mostly (and almost by definition) used for fun, and sometimes to defuse tensions with mock abuse. Pay particular attention to the tone of voice.

Slang is the yeast that good communicators use to leaven the dough of officialese. Slang is a sure way to get your message across. Slang is the language we use when we are relaxed and with friends or colleagues. It is our wordplay. Everyone and every walk of life have its own slang. For instance, in the hospitality business, or "hospo" as the Kiwis call it, we all have our own terminology which binds us together. In the kitchen if you are regarded by your colleagues as a bit of an idiot then you will be called a 'doughnut' by your fellow chefs. On the front of house we have something called "The 86 List". There are many other instances where slang could be used.

GLOSSARY OF KIWI SLANG

A

A into G   Arse into gear, usually intended to advise hurry up.

AB's, The   The All Blacks.

Afghan   A popular biscuit made with cocoa powder.

Aftermatch   A boozy celebration after the game, mostly of the sporty kind, usually restricted to males.

Afto/arvo   Afternoon.

All around
the houses   All over the place.

All Blacks   The New Zealand National Rugby Union team, from the colour of the strip and said to be from a printer's error: a Daily Mail reporter wrote of a match played on 11 October 1905, won 63–0 by New Zealand, that the whole team played with precision and speed as if they were "all backs", printed as "all blacks".

All done up
like a sore toe   Disparaging reference to someone overdressed and over impressed with it.

Amber fluid/liquid   Beer.

Angus   Angry, as in Angus bull.

Antipodes, The   The name attributed to both Australia and New Zealand.

Anzac   Acronym for the Australian and New Zealand Army Corps from WW1.

Anzac biscuit   Firm, teeth–challenging biscuit made with oats.

Aratanic   Nickname for a Cook Strait ferry which kept breaking down in recent years, mercifully not to the extent of the Titanic.

Aroha job   Work done for love, not money.

Artesian Fresian   Watered–down milk.

Australian haka   A transparent attempt to avoid paying your way, developed in a television ad in which a group of drinkers inform one it is his turn to pay for a round. He pats pockets vigorously and then whines "Where's me flamin' wallet?"

B

Bach	From early 1900s a weekend or holiday hut or cottage by the sea or lake or in the wilderness.
Bag	To disparage or 'knock' someone.
Barber, The	A keen wind, especially that scything out of the gorge into Greymouth on the West Coast.
Barbie	The barbecue, which is pretty much an antipodean necessity.
Barn Dance, The	Diagonally–striped pedestrian crossing.
Bathers	Swimming costume.
Beach, The	The name for the entire holiday area by the sea in New Zealand.
Beehive, The	Cone–shaped concrete parliamentary building in Wellington designed for the New Zealand cabinet and staff by Sir Basil Spence.
Big Wet, The	Continuous downpour for days, so–called by Aucklanders rightly fearful it will spoil sporting fixtures.
Biodegradable Poms	Kiwis, as described by Aussies.
Black Caps	National Men's Cricket team.
Black Ferns	National Women's Rugby team.
Blenheimers	Loss of memory from too much wine. A play on Alzheimer's disease and Blenheimer wine.
Bogan	Idiot or misfit.
Bonza/bonzer	Pleasing or well–regarded.
Booai/booay/ boohai	A remote place.
Booze barn	A large tavern with ready access fro consumption of alcohol, popular in 1970's.
Bottle store/shop	A retail outlet which sells alcohol.
Bowser	Petrol station or pump.
Bro	A friendly greeting, short for 'brother'.
Bungy	Elastic cord.

Bush	Forest or rural area.
BYO	Bring Your Own, usually refers to wine.

C

Cake Tin, The   Nickname for the new millenium stadium on the former railyards in downtown Wellington. Used for international/national rugby matches and concerts. Home of the Wellington Hurricanes.

Capital of Cow Country	Hamilton.
Cathedral City	Christchurch.
Chateau Cardboard	Cheap bulk wine or bag in box.
Chateau Taranaki	Beer.
Cher bro	Excellent, to a contemporary youth.
Chilly bin	Insulated plastic container for carrying food and drink.
Choice	Excellent
Chook	Chicken.
City of Sails	Auckland.
Cooking with gas	A fast solution or ready to get going.
Corker	Anything appreciated.
Cracker	Rated highly
Crash hot!	Exclamation of strong approval.
Crib	Holiday cottage in the South Island (e.g. a bach)
Crook	Ill or angry.
Cuz/cuzzy/ cuzzy bro	Polynesian male greeting.

D

Damper	Basic bush bread made from flour and water and cooked in the ashes of an open fire.
Dingbat	Crazy or eccentric person.
Dinkum	Fair, genuine or reliable.

Ditch, The	The Tasman Sea (across the Ditch is Australia).
Drongo	Stupid or clumsy fellow.
Dunny	A toilet.
Durry	A cigarette, specifically roll–your–own.

E

Eh?	Interrogative or emphasising add–on at the end of sentences e.g. "We really put it to the Aussie cricketers, eh?"

F

Floater	A meat pie floating in gravy.
Full of puha	Talking nonsense.

G

G'day	Hello.
Get off the grass!	Scornful rejection.
Good on ya/you	Well done.
Good–oh!	Moderate approval.
Gutless wonder	Poorly performed person or thing.

H

Half–pie	Unimpressive, poorly performed, not done properly.
Hard yakker	Demanding work, usually manual labour.
Hooker	Plays wearing number 2 jersey in Rugby Union and is responsible for hooking the ball in the scrum and throwing it in to the rest of the pack of forwards in a line–out.
Hoon	Hooligan or ruffian.
Humdinger	Anything attractive.

I

I'll see you right   To look after someone.
Invincibles, The   The legendary 1924 All Blacks, who won every game on their Northern Hemisphere tour.

J

Jafa   An Aucklander, as in the acronym "Just Another Effin' Aucklander"
Jandal   Flip–flop or sandal.

K

Kai   A meal, from Maori for 'food'
Kia Ora   G'day or hello.
Kiwi style   The way New Zealanders are expected to behave, which is modest, rsolute, resourceful, no boasting.

L

L&P   Lemon and Paeroa, a popular soft drink made originally from Paeroa mineral water.
Log, The/
Log O'Wood   The Ranfurly Shield, interprovincial rugby trophy. The log holder is the rugby province currently holding the shield.

M

Mainland, The   The South Island.
Maori Magna Carta Treaty of Waitangi.
Mountain oysters   Sheep's testicles, a delicacy for some.

N

Number 8   The forward at the back of the Rugby Union scrum.

O

OE   Overseas Experience, which young Kiwis get, often on a working holiday and equivalent to the "Gap Year".

Old Country, The   The place immigrants left behind, usually British Isles

Oriental Parade   The well-to-do of Wellington, who live in the swanky inner suburb of Oriental Bay around Cable Street.

P

Paekakariki
Express, The   Nick-name of famously quick All Black winger Christian Cullen.

Palmie   Palmerston North.

Pav   Pavlova meringue cake, which is arguably the nation's most famous dessert.

Phat   Fashionable or trendy.

Pom   A person from Britain.

Q

Quad   Four-wheeled motorised farm bike that has replaced the horse.

R

Rack off!   Go Away!

Roto-Vegas   Rotorua.

S

Shout	Round of drinks, as in "It's my shout!"
Silver Ferns	National Women's netball team.
Slab	24 pack carton of beer.
Sleepy Hollow	Nelson.
Southerly	A biting cold wind.
Stubbie	A small bottle of beer.
Sulphur City	Rotorua.

Super 14   Rugby competition between 14 conglomerate provincial teams from South Africa, Australia and New Zealand.

Sweet as   Strong approval.

T

TAB   Totalisator Agency Board, state–run betting shop.

Tall poppy   Outstanding individual who has aroused the envy of lesser achievers.

Taranaki bullshit   Boasting.

Tight Five, The   The five forwards who bind the rugby scrum, namely the hooker, the two props in front, behind them two locks.

Tiki–Tour   A quick trip around the tourist highlights of an area.

Turn on
the Waipouri   Switch on the electricity, from an Otago river damned for hydro electric power.

U

Up the Mokau   Very lost, as you would be up this very remote North Taranaki river

Ute   Utility truck or van.

W

Woop woops   Remote place. Often said in the/out in the woop woops.

"Despite having been an ex pat for more than two decades I still consider myself very much a Kiwi. But maybe because I don't live in New Zealand I hold my country and its wine to very high standards. I had a (restaurant) client say to me once, with a smile: "there's rather a lot of Kiwi wines on the new wine list…" I replied that was because they were good AND suitable for his wine list. I told him he didn't pay me to be patriotic but to do the best job I could. I guess that sums up my attitude. I genuinely think New Zealand deserves more than one listing (Marlborough Sauvignon) on any kind of ambitious list. I think the key is natural acidity: it brings freshness, or refreshment, if you prefer and hence real drinkability."

Peter McCombie MW - wine consultant

"UK consumers, especially Londoners don't realise how lucky they are now with such a high quality of coffee that is readily available"
Richard Reed - Co-owner Nude Espresso Coffee Roasters

To watch this roving sommelier video, please scan QR code with your smartphone

KIWIS ABROAD

KIWIS ABROAD

Over the years, not only have I come to realise that New Zealanders are generally lovely people, but also the fact that, like me, they enjoy travelling. I have met many during life's journey, either through my working in restaurants, bars and hotels or whenever they have been on their own "Big OE". Apart from seeing various photos of family, at the tender age of ten, good old David James was the first Kiwi I ever encountered and I have met many more since.

For instance, go into many bars and restaurants, and now coffee shops, especially within particular suburbs of London and I guarantee that you will encounter a Kiwi at some stage. Chances are you will probably be served by one, and possibly the chef who prepares your meal or a person working behind the scenes is a Kiwi. Since the mid-2000s they have completely galvanised the coffee culture in this country. We all know what a 'flat white' is now and even some well-known multi-national brands have latched onto it. These caffeine artisans who give us our daily fix really care about what they do. Great quality coffee and New Zealand go hand in hand. The baristas who work over here (the majority of them are Antipodeans) pride themselves in their profession and the quality of their product and training. When you visit New Zealand you will discover that bad coffee, especially with regards to product quality and the service of it, is completely unacceptable. Let us be honest, before the Kiwis and Aussies came to London, with the exception of Monmouth Coffee Roasters and a couple of others, the quality of coffee in the capital was pretty diabolical. Some well-known chains continue to sell overpriced bland coffee, topped up with a dollop of warmish milk and charge mega-bucks for absolute rubbish. Passionate individuals such as Richard Reed has grabbed the coffee industry with the same spirit as a Richie McCaw tackle and has become one of the leading lights of third wave coffee.

For me, these grafters are the unsung heroes. These people go about their profession each day with love and care are the real champions. Nowadays we put so much emphasis on food, especially with how it looks and its provenance, probably even more so than how it actually tastes. That possibly goes the same for wine too. Allegedly, as consumers, we are made to feel we should order particular wines in restaurants or compelled to purchase them in retail outlets because "society dictates", yet without actually knowing how they taste. For most people the main criteria for wine is: Will I like it? Can I afford it? Will it go with what I am eating? Yes these factors are very important, but when you get down to it essentially it is all about people. Good food and good wine and experiences are all about people. This requires time, patience and trust, yet without humans and these relationships, we would not have a food and wine culture.

Before we get stuck into some more anecdotes, I would like to pay tribute to some well-travelled Kiwis, most of whom are now living and working in the UK or elsewhere. They have done many positive things to enlighten our culture and enrich our lives.

Margaret Harvey MW; Robyn Wilson; Emily MacDonald; Fleur McCree; Sara and Tim Fogarty; Misha and Andy Wilkinson; Nicki Mansfield; Nicky Cranswick; Kathy Sturge; Frances Durcan; Chantelle Nicholson; Peter McCombie MW; Warren Adamson; Sam Harrop MW; Michael Seresin; Michael Clark; Michael Connolly; Brett Woonton; Andrew Connor; Pete Connell; Peter Lorimer; Nick Demurgue; Sam Lockyer; Jayson Bryant; John Bartlett; Hayden Johnston; Riki Hutchinson; Liam Kelleher; Bernard Budel; Aaron Stott; Nick Watt; Hamish Brown; Miles Kirby and the Caravan team; Richard Reed and the Nude Espresso team; Michael Allpress; Mat Follas; Anna Hansen, Candi Giachetti and The Modern Pantry team; Adam Wills and the Kopapa team; Susan and Tom Glynn and the Suze in Mayfair team; Cristian Hossack; Sophie Uddin; Melanie Brown (nee Ellis); Nicola Wood; Lorraine Martin; Michael McGrath; Peter Gordon and The Providores team. Of course now it is so easy to keep in touch via Facebook and Twitter too. Don't be a stranger!

Misha Wilkinson lives with her husband Andy in Singapore. The couple own a vineyard (aptly named Misha's Vineyard) in Central Otago. I first met them in 2010 at a wine tasting at New Zealand House. I am a big fan of their wines and also attended a wine maker dinner at The Providores Restaurant. Misha's Vineyard is located on one of the most spectacular sites in New Zealand. Situated on the edge of Lake Dunstan, the 57-hectare estate is in the Bendigo sub-region of Central Otago. They have employed a world-class wine maker Olly Masters and a world-class viticulturist Robin Dicey to ensure that you get to enjoy fabulous wines in each and every bottle. I am particularly fond of their aromatic whites (Riesling, Pinot Gris and Gewurztraminer) and their award-winning Pinot Noir is not too shabby either.

Here is their story, which she told us at the dinner: "When we started this adventure our objective was to create something really special and our motto was, and will always be, 'no compromises'. Already we have discovered so much. We've discovered how special this region of Central Otago really is, we've also discovered some amazing things about the unique piece of land we chose for our vineyard, and we're constantly discovering things about growing the best grapes and making the best wines. This is the most ambitious adventure we've ever taken and we hope you enjoy being part of it."

"Back in the late 1800s many Chinese immigrants joined the gold rush in Central Otago as they had in California, Australia and elsewhere. The neatly stacked gold tailings in the gullies are the remnants of their alluvial mining and the crumbling remains of stone miners' cottages are evidence of a tough existence on this land. Most of these Chinese prospectors came from the countryside of Canton in southern China – some 10,000 kilometres away. And like all pioneering history, the story of how they endured the harsh conditions of this rugged landscape to find their fortunes in the most southern goldfields of the world, is a remarkable story of adversity and adaptation. Finding this perfect location on which to establish Misha's Vineyard was the first milestone in our journey"

At the wine dinner Misha continued to enlighten us with the story of the Lucky Number 8: "In Chinese culture the number "8" is considered the luckiest of numbers, representing prosperity and good fortune. It was fortuitous to realise the Misha's Vineyard was located on State Highway 8, just 8 kilometres from the nearest town of Cromwell, and on the land that was originally known as Sheep Run 238 when it was part of the old Morven Hills Station. On the vineyard 8 clones of Pinot Noir have been planted in two row directions – 288 degrees on the slopes and lakefront terrace and 341 degrees (adding up to 8) on the higher terraces. The first vintage from Misha's Vineyard was 2008. At our ground-breaking ceremony, we placed a Chinese coin beneath our first 8 planted vines to symbolically return the 'old gold' to the ground and bring luck for the 'new gold'. A replica of this gold coin, acting as our logo, is placed on the capsule of each bottle. You may say this is a kind of vineyard 'feng-shui'."

I interviewed Misha for my blog and asked what her 'desert island' dish and wine pairing would be. You will find the recipe for Misha's favourite dish later and you may wish to try it.

I have enjoyed many meals at Anna Hansen's restaurant The Modern Pantry in Clerkenwell, London. Two wine dinners in particular spring to mind: Mahi with Brian Bicknell in 2010 and Pegasus Bay with Ed Donaldson in 2011. I have admired her special type of fusion cuisine and those wines for a while. Subsequently, I have returned to her restaurant many times since, including a sumptuous lunch of Rieslings and the staff, led by Candi Giachetti, always provide me with a warm welcome.

Two stand out food and wine pairings from those gastronomic feasts were: Guinea fowl 'mole rojo', plantain and tomatillo paired with the elegant Mahi Pinot Noir and the beetroot, crab and avocado with the zesty Pegasus Bay Waipara Riesling. I met a couple of people from Christchurch one of whom, Greg used to work at Oxo Tower and is head chef at The Wells gastro pub in Primrose Hill. Small world…eh? Anna has very kindly supplied me with a few of her recipes, which can be found in the index at the back of the book. You see my friends I have not just been gallivanting around in vain wasting my time, as all of this 'research' is totally for your benefit. Rest assured, stick with me as your friendly sommelier and tour guide on this journey and I will guarantee you maximum satisfaction!

I mentioned earlier that I started to 'specialise' in New Zealand wines back in the 1990s. During my time at Oxo Tower, I became good friends with Peter McCombie MW. In fact, over the years not only do we regularly keep in touch and have tasted and judged many wines together, but also I have always regarded Peter as a bit of a mentor. I attended the NZ Winegrowers wine tastings on a regular basis. Back then, Katharine O'Callaghan was at the helm in London and I met her two assistants, Alison Power and Charlotte Rushworth. They have always been very helpful and supportive towards me. Stand out memories include their various tastings and events, especially when hosted up in the Penthouse at NZ House on Haymarket. The views from there are amazing, and the team always continue to impress with its professionalism and innovation when it comes to the tastings. In addition, speaking as a sommelier, it is always refreshing to discover the effort which is put in and the emphasis they place on the food-matching element. Several years ago, I recall going to a master class, when they paired various Kiwi wines with different dishes. One pairing was a cold rice pudding with vanilla and mango which was served with a dry sparkling wine. This worked surprisingly well because the dry, biscuity flavour of the wine together with the bubbles refreshed the palate and balanced up the sweetness in the fruity and creamy dessert. For me it was a revelation and showed real attention to detail.

I have a recipe from my own repertoire and I use it whenever I am in the mood to re-create that rice pudding experience.

Here are a couple of anecdotes which Katherine would like to share: "I was appointed UK Marketing Manager for what was then known as the Wine Institute of New Zealand in July 1999. Already an enthusiastic consumer of New Zealand Sauvignon Blanc, this was a dream role for me and one that did not disappoint. Anne-Marie McKenzie from the Wine Institute of New Zealand's head office in Auckland, organised an unforgettable whistle-stop tour of all the main wine regions –Auckland, Matakana, Waiheke Island, Gisborne, Hawkes Bay, Wairarapa, Marlborough, Nelson, Waipara, Martinborough, Canterbury and Central Otago, Incredibly, we covered all of this ground in just eight days. Looking back now, I don't know how we did it but I remember there was a lot of driving and a few slightly hairy domestic flights involved. Everyone was so welcoming and the famous New Zealand 'can-do' attitude really bowled me over. I met so many amazing person-alities on the trip. I must have visited over 40 wineries and tasted hundreds of fantastic wines over those eight days and each region had its own appeal. It's so difficult to single out one highlight of the trip although I remember that on my return, it was the beauti-fully haunting landscape of Waipara that lingered longest in my memory.

I ate at so many fantastic wineries and restaurants and the gastronomic heaven that is Sileni Estates in Hawkes Bay deserves a special mention, but ironically, after all this time, the culinary experience that most stands out for me was at a modest beach café, somewhere on the Kaikoura coast (en route from Blenheim to Waipara with Anne-Marie McKenzie). It was one of those perfect moments – clear blue skies, a warm sea breeze, dolphins playing out at sea, deliciously fresh fish and chips and a classic, full-on, New Zealand 'Savvy'. I can still remember the delicious combi-nation to this day. Another moment that stands out is at the end of a very long week travelling around New Zealand, taking the ferry to the beautifully laid-back Waiheke Island on a scorching hot, sunny day. After visiting various wineries, Elmira, who used to work at the Wine Institute of New Zealand in Auckland, took us to her 'batch' (holiday chalet) and suggested we all go for a swim in the sea. She managed to rustle up an old swimsuit for me which looked as though it had last been used in the 50s. The sea was so refreshing and after our dip, we ate fresh fish cooked on a makeshift barbecue and shared a bottle of Neill Culley's Cable Bay Sauvignon Blanc whilst enjoying the stunning views out to sea. Bliss."

When Katharine left New Zealand Winegrowers (she went on to create her own PR company) Warren Adamson took over the role as Director. I admire and like Warren (a.k.a Wazza) very much. With him, nothing ever seems to be a problem and over the years I have found him very friendly and approachable. In 2009, when Wazza left that position he went on to work for Craggy Range as Marketing Director. David Cox (the person who I video interviewed for the foreword) took over from him and became Director of New Zealand Winegrowers (Europe) based in London. He left this position towards the end of 2012.

One night I had an amazing experience with Wazza. TJ Peabody from Craggy Range was in town and they hosted a wine dinner at Hix Restaurant in Soho. Various Craggy Range wines flowed without limit and there was a never ending stream of food. The menu was called "The Beefy Feast" and we were in for a treat. To be honest, I found our hosts' generosity quite over-whelming, yet of course, very much appreciated it. By the end of the evening I certainly realised what a top-flight outfit they are with an excellent range of wines, which deserve top-notch food. My main highlights were the smoked salmon with the "Kidnap-per's" Chardonnay and the selection of different bovine cuts, ranging from ribs, oxtail, rib-eye and porterhouse steaks with "Calvert Vineyard" Pinot Noir from Central Otago and "Block 14" Gimblett Gravels Syrah. Nowadays, to get hold of smoked salmon and beef is quite straight forward, but I would suggest you buy what you can afford and not skimp on quality. There are some great quality butchers still practising their craft in the UK and as for the salmon the very best I have ever tasted is from Hansen & Lydersen in Stoke Newington, London. Try it and you won't be disappointed.

I absolutely adore Bakewell tart and the enormous one served to us at that dinner at Hix was an epic. Inspired by this, I have tried to re-create that whole experience a few times by making an effort to bake one myself. There is a nice standby from a good friend Jess Latchford of Secrett's Direct in the recipe chapter.

Another highlight of my epicurean odyssey was when

Tim Heath of Cloudy Bay came over to London. I went to the headquarters of Moet & Hennessy in Belgravia and interviewed him for my blog. It was also a great pleasure to be invited to attend two wonderful dinners: The Providores and The Montagu Restaurant inside the Hyatt Regency – The Churchill Hotel on Portman Square. The latter created and hosted a Cloudy Bay-sponsored chef's table right in front of the kitchen in the heart of the restaurant with a special bespoke menu. My favourite dish of that dinner prepared by Carlos Teixeira was the whole roasted foie gras with Cox Orange Pippins and truffle. The dish was paired with the barrel-fermented Sauvignon Blanc "Te Koko". At first when I saw the menu, the dish and its wine pairing concerned me and I thought it would not work. However it worked surprisingly well and tasted sublime, even though extremely decadent. The rich texture of the foie gras, the sweetness and acidity of the apple and the earthy aromatics of the truffle married beautifully with the complex and powerful, yet fresh and elegant 2007 Cloudy Bay "Te Koko". Try it whenever you are feeling in an indulgent mood. Tim Heath continues: "For me there is nothing better than packing a bottle of Kiwi Pinot in my pack and heading into the hills for a "tramp". After a big day's hiking through the mountains, nothing beats a glass of wine on the doorstep of an old "back-country" hut watching the sun dip below the skyline before a meal in front of a crackling fireplace – especially if the meal involves a bit of wild venison." There are oodles more food and wine pairings and my roving sommelier videos in the index and web links sections. I hope you feel inspired.

By now you might have gathered that I am a bit of a fan of The Providores Restaurant and Tapa Room in Marylebone. In fact, I have become a bit of a 'regular' there. During 2010, when I was researching material for this book, I attended many wine dinners which they hosted on a monthly basis. These events were the brain-child of Melanie Brown (nee Ellis), the restaurant's talented wine buyer and beverage operations manager. I She has compiled a choice selection of New Zealand wines that really displays the diversity of what the country has to offer.

I have interviewed Melanie on more than one occasion: "We pride ourselves not only on sourcing many different varietals throughout, but by also selecting wines from regions that showcase the diversity in each sub-region's terroir." Personally I believe that one of the main strengths of the selection, apart from this diversity and regionality of New Zealand wines, is the range offered by-the-glass. Melanie continued: "With a constantly changing by the glass and carafe list, we can give our customers the opportunity to taste and explore the country's most current wines. What we are ultimately trying to achieve here is to offer our customers something different – to show them that New Zealand is not just about Marlborough and Sauvignon Blanc."

Ok, so you have heard the sales and marketing 'schpiel'. You are genuinely fascinated by the 'story'. You have never actually made the very long schlep over to New Zealand to be able to visualise the vineyards, yet they look so idyllic in the brochure. However, when you get down to it, for me, the 'acid test' is how the wines actually taste. Most importantly, as a sommelier, I think of how the wines will perform when put up against food. Which dishes would be the best to bring out the flavours in the food and help assist the wines to fully express themselves? Will these 'modern classic New World' wines cope well with intricate and flavoursome cuisines or be better suited to more simple dishes? Will the tastes and flavours complement and enhance each other? Will they clash brutally like two vinous bulls in a china shop, or be a perfect harmonious marriage dancing on your taste buds? Throw into the mix Peter Gordon's eclectic-fusion style of cooking and you have a real challenge.

Many chefs just seem to throw a few ingredients together without any sense of coherence or connection and hope that the tastes and flavours will blend together. However, let us face it, most of the time they end up as complete disasters on the plate and 'confusion cuisine'. I can safely say that I have never had a culinary disaster at The Providores. Peter and his team of chefs have drawn from all their influences of travels around Europe, Mediterranean, Middle East and Asia. When you read through the menu, you think that is never going to work. Yet when you taste the food, not only does it have such personality, but also it actually is exquisite and balanced. These are all thoughts and challenging decisions which go through the minds of the chef and sommelier. When it comes to the fine art of food and wine pairing, there is no better team in London than chefs Peter Gordon and Cristian Hossack and sommelier Melanie Brown. Being married to a chef (Hamish Brown of Roka fame), Mel perhaps does have a slight advantage. Together, they are really impressive and this requires great understanding, skill and attention to detail. Most importantly they go about their craft in a focused, yet down-to-earth and unstuffy way. Allegedly, they are not interested in formality or Michelin stars, as their priority is to ensure that their guests are comfortable. They must be doing something right, as people return to have their tastebuds titillated and enjoy the buzzing ambience, time and time again. The floor staff are always friendly and play an integral part in the restaurant's success.

Here's a snapshot of some favourite highlights of food and wine pairings from those wine dinners at The Providores during 2010. There's a load more stuff in the back too!

Salad of crispy belly pork and green papaya with lychees and tamarind caramel dressing
2007 Seresin "Chiaroscuro", Marlborough

Roast venison with horseradish beetroot arancini, bok choy and bone marrow sauce
2005 Vin Alto "Ritorno", Clevedon, Auckland

Roast New Zealand farmed venison on bok choy and sesame cucumber with satay sauce and smoked chilli jelly
2008 Staete Landt Syrah, Marlborough

AN EPICUREAN ODYSSEY

Apple and feijoa pie with palm sugar ice cream
2008 Staete Landt Riesling "Auslese", Marlborough

Galangal and smoked coconut laksa with soba noodles and a
Tiger prawn
2008 Pegasus Bay "Bel Canto" Riesling, Waipara

Pressed ham hock and water chestnut terrine with wok-fried
mange tout, green mango and pickled bean-sprouts and
pineapple sweet and sour dressing
2009 Man O'War "Valhalla" Chardonnay, Waiheke Island

Caramelised pork belly with confit parsnip, nashi pear,
umeboshi and candied walnuts
2007 Cloudy Bay Chardonnay, Marlborough

Palm sugar custard square with salted caramel sauce, hazelnuts
and clotted cream
2007 Cloudy Bay Late-harvest Riesling, Marlborough

Tempura battered Kaipara Harbour oyster on pickled papaya,
coriander and salted coconut milk salad with ginger, garlic and
black bean crumbs
2010 Tinpot Hut Gruner Veltliner, Marlborough

Smoked halibut with broad beans, golden beets and nori sauce
2009 Escarpment Chardonnay, Martinborough

Tagliatelle with cep cream, Pecorino and Perigord truffle
2008 "Kiwa by Escarpment" Pinot Noir, Martinborough

Tandoori prawn with tomato sambal and galangal coconut
sauce
2009 Misha's Vineyard "Dress Circle" Pinot Gris, Central Otago

Over the years, Peter Gordon has had many protégés and colleagues, who have gone on to achieve their own success. These include Anna Hansen and Miles Kirby amongst many others. As mentioned earlier the people 'behind the scenes' are the unsung heroes. For me, the person at The Providores who entirely epitomises this role is Cristian Hossack (a.k.a Crisso). He is a very talented chef and a real culinary magician. However, he is a very humble chap, who has modestly shunned the limelight because of his down-to-earth nature and personality. What he lacks in typical arrogant 'cheffy' ego, he certainly makes up for in his honest and confident cooking. He was there for six years in total. He took over the head chef position from Miles Kirby in 2009, who went on to set up Caravan in Exmouth Market. Crisso has very kindly contributed a recipe from his repertoire. As you will see by the quantity of ingredients and technical elements it is quite a challenging dish to make. You will find it in the recipe section, naturally. As mentioned in the Auckland chapter, you will now find him cooking up a storm on Waiheke Island.

From time to time, I like to meet up with my Kiwi friends who also live in London. Fleur McCree co-owns Little Beauty, a bespoke vineyard in the Waihopai Valley in Marlborough, which produces elegant and expressive wines. This is their story

"With us, individuality is where it's at – so we needed a name to match. This sense of individuality is also reflected in everything we do – in the vineyard and the cellar – making for distinctive wines with heaps of personality. In the Antipodes, the term Little Beauty is a phrase often used as a term of endearment, or when one feels excited about something. Positive connotation all the way! You've all seen Peter Jackson's Lord of the Rings ...and yup...that's exactly what it looks like in New Zealand (only minus the Hobbits and Orks). Incredibly beautiful and dramatic scenery. A bit like our wines – 'dramatically beautiful'. Plus we're a little nation (less than 4 million of us)...and of course, we're only a little company." Their ethos is: "I'm proudly Kiwi and I'm a Little Beauty"

Another Kiwi who has become a good friend is Sam Lockyer. Currently, he is working in Melbourne in Australia, but he used to be Brand Ambassador for Forrest wines. We used to meet up frequently and put a few wines through their paces, including an exciting 'head to head' tasting with NZ v The Rest of The World. I love aromatic white varietals and Dr John Forrest, amongst others, is leading the way experimenting with Riesling, Gewurztraminer, Arneis and Gruner Veltliner. They also produce some excellent quality reds, especially Syrah and Bordeaux blends from the Gimblett Gravels part of Hawke's Bay.

I interviewed Sam for my blog, which as you may be aware also features a few hundred roving sommelier videos and my wine reviews and tasting notes. We had quite a bit of fun too. After all, food and wine pairing can be quite intimidating, yet should never be taken too seriously. We also hosted an epic event at L'Atelier des Chefs cookery school in Marylebone and a few wine tastings at various branches of Adnams on our little 'roadshow' together. Before coming over to England, Sam spent some time gaining experience within the wine industry in New Zealand. The people, who have inspired and mentored him along the way, as well as Dr John Forrest, include wine makers David Knappstein and Chris Andrew, with whom he worked during his vintage experience at Forrest Estate. Robin and Matt Dicey of Mt Difficulty and John Atkinson MW have also proved influential, especially with a shared love of Pinot Noir and Burgundy. We picked a few dishes off the Providores' menu and tasted the wines to see how they would work. I thought the belly pork dish with the 2006 "John Forrest Collection" The White was the best combination. I did not know this, but apparently famous wine writer Matthew Jukes was the instigator behind the wine.

As Dr John Forrest himself says: "New Zealand has an enviable international reputation for single varietal white wines but to date, few wine makers have explored white blends. In my winemaking experience, I have found the whole is often greater than the sum of the parts and The White is my expression of this belief. To achieve this, I have chosen from my vineyards only those varieties which have won acclaim in that region. From the warm, stony Gimblett Gravels in Hawke's Bay – Viognier; from the limestone soils of North

Otago – Pinot Gris; from Central Otago – Pinot Gris and Riesling; and from Marlborough's patchwork of riverbed soils – Sauvignon Blanc, Riesling, Chardonnay, Chenin Blanc, and Gewürztraminer. The final blend will vary from year to year and may not contain all varietals, depending on my judgment as to the contribution each part makes to the whole."

To tell you the truth, I did not really like it when I first tasted it around four years ago. I thought the wine was a little bit on the shy side. This complex wine requires patience and time to develop. Each individual component needs to express itself and the 2006 is beautiful right now. A little sommelier tip – decant this aromatic white wine and do not serve it too cold, as you will lose the flavour. The 2007 vintage is also drinking nicely now.

I am very fond of scallops. I love cooking and eating them and like to add some salty, piquant speck or spicy chorizo and a squeeze of lemon to finish. I also love experimenting, especially when cooking, but my main aim is to see which wine would be the best combination. Owing to my passion for Riesling, especially those with some bottle age, I like to taste a line up of Kiwi wines which I have in my cellar. The delicious, toasty lime marmalade and grapefruit oil-scented 2001 Forrest "The Valleys" Wairau Limited Release Riesling from Marlborough with seared plump and juicy scallops was utterly sublime. Talk about mouth-watering and who says that New World Rieslings cannot age? There are a few blog articles for you in the back.

All of these bacchanalian shenanigans during 2010 culmi-nated with an amazing climax. Peter Gordon and Michael McGrath decided to host a huge Providores 'Pop Up' restaurant at The Village Underground in Shoreditch. It was one of the best experiences of my life. In my role as "Roving Sommelier", I took along my camera and recorded the event on video. I have some amazing footage, including interviews featured on my You Tube channel and website. How the team managed to pull off such a culinary spectacle was incredible, especially as the dinner was for 160 guests and included four courses and 14 wines. It was a real Kiwi showcase and the hottest ticket of the year.

I found that over the course of these dinners, I always learned something new each time. For example, I did not have a clue about kikones and tamari before I met Peter Gordon! But with wine it is such a valuable experience when you have the person who made them or a vineyard representative actually standing there in the room presenting their wines with passion. Yes, we can all engage and have the opportunity to ask the expert "Errm, how much new French oak has been used?" or learn "This wine has spent a certain part of its life going through a malo-lactic fermentation" and so on, yet do we really wish to be bombarded with all that 'technical' information. Will it actually enhance your dining experience and is it relevant? Will you enjoy your meal even more by knowing the fact that the wine has been cool-fermented in stainless steel tanks? Probably not. When we are in a restaurant environment, why are we compelled to 'test' the sommelier with seemingly awkward questions, which perhaps do not even matter? Please note my dear readers, I will always refer to the very minimum, if any, technical information in my blog articles, tasting notes and reviews, because I feel that for most people it is far too intimidating. I want to help make wines accessible, not try to put people down or make them feel ignorant. Let us not get hung up about wine scores either! One thing is clear though, New Zealand wines have remained focused and consistent and in time will continue to develop more expression and complexity. Aromatic whites, Pinot Noirs and Syrah are definitely on the up, especially with regards to certain regions. I would passionately encourage you to look out for them in your wine merchants and restaurants.

For me, when it comes to wine, it is all about sharing, inter-action, conviviality and enjoyment. There is a story in every bottle. Most importantly these occasions are all about the food, the wine, the people and those experiences. That is the beauty of food and wine and it can be a real education. It certainly has been for me, especially ever since 1996, when not only did I decide to come to London to live and work, but also to specialise my career in food and wine and become a sommelier. Now we are blessed with such an array and variety of excellent wine bars, retailers and merchants. For instance, look no further than Vinoteca in London. Kiwi Brett Woonton and co-owner of this award-winning, mini restaurant chain opened their first branch in Farringdon in 2005. They currently have four successful operations in London (Farringdon, Marylebone, Soho and Chiswick), with more to follow and are leading the way with their convivial, wine-focused eateries. The food is gutsy and honest and they have arguably one of the best value for money wine lists in town. Also in London, one of the new kids on the wine block is fellow Kiwi Liam Kelleher, who owns a wine shop called "Noble Fine Liquor" in trendy Hackney. He opened in late 2012, hosts regular wine tastings and has a really interesting range of wines on offer. He loves craft beer too.

1996 was also the year Peter Gordon came onto my radar. In 2001, the year he created The Providores in Marylebone, I was working as head sommelier for legendary chef Pierre Koffmann. I remember the wonderful work Peter did as being an integral part of the annual "Leuka Charity Dinner" hosted at The Berkeley Hotel in Knightsbridge. So before I round off this part of my Kiwi odyssey, I would like to give a few final words to Peter who would like to share one of his memorable experiences of New Zealand and give us an insight into how it all got started.

Peter Gordon, co-owner of The Providores & Tapa Room, has been experimenting with ingredients and techniques from around the world for most of his career, but for a long time he had no idea what to call the hybrid style of cooking he had created. "When I ran the kitchen at the Sugar Club in Notting Hill in the 1990s, in one week Time Out voted us best Modern British restaurant and Fay Maschler in the Standard gave us an Eros Award for best Pacific Rim restaurant," he says. "That made me think, what are we? It was just food that was personal to me, the food that I'd always loved cooking. Then I read about this guy in the States called Norman Van Aken who was doing what he called fusion food, and I thought, ah fusion, that sounds good, I'll use that term."

Peter continues..."I've been a fan of NZ wines even from those terrible days in the late 1970s of badly made and overly sweet Muller Thurgau and Moselle. I even went to university to become a wine maker, but instead embarked on my lifetime love of cooking. However in 2005 I was able to combine both when I became a partner with 3 others in a vineyard in the Waitaki Valley, in the fledgling grape growing area of North Otago. My partners were the much-lauded wine maker Michelle Richardson, my partner at the time Michael McGrath and Auckland businessman, and owner of the land, Steve Cozens. We launched the vineyard with a canapé party – although it was spoken about for years after because of the amazing location and the food I cooked. Michael and I had flown out from London with an Irish journalist in tow and landed, via Air New Zealand and a hire car, the day before the party. Jet-lagged and a bit pushed for time, I was able to work with the assembled folk, organised by a local organic honey producer, Kate White, and cook a huge selection of canapés using locally sourced food, which we served on the banks of the pristine Waitaki River. The river flows from the top of Aoraki, the tallest mountain in New Zealand, also known as Mt Cook. It passes east through several huge and beautiful lakes, coloured milky turquoise from the schist it contains. It wends it way along a braided riverbed until it hits the east coast between Timaru and Oamaru.

We ate salmon from the river, served with grated wasabi which grew on the riverbank. Rabbits (local pests in their millions at times) were dispatched in baby pies made by the local baker to my recipe. Locally farmed Merino sheep were roasted in chunks; local plums were rolled in thinly sliced farmed venison which had been coated in spices. Organic honey was baked into dessert canapés and all of it was served on the banks of the icy cold blue flowing river, near the bridge made famous in the classic and iconic NZ movie Goodbye Pork Pie. Since then, the small band of youthful Waitaki Valley vineyards have been producing small amounts of highly-rated varietals, with our own Waitaki Braids producing Pinot Noir, Pinot Gris, Riesling and a 100% Pinot Noir Rosé. Jancis Robinson MW rated our inaugural 2004 Pinot Noir highly enough to say Waitaki Braids had the potential to become a classic vineyard of the future – one of only 9 vineyards that she said this about. Pretty good, eh!"

Finally, to conclude this chapter and collection of "Kiwis Abroad" anecdotes on a positive note, someone special deserves a mention. I first met Nicki Mansfield in 2007 when we visited Egon Muller's vineyards in Germany together. Right from the get-go, she came across as being a lovely person. Indeed she is. However, unfortunately we lost contact and she returned home to New Zealand. During my 'break' when I left Orrery in 2009 and went travelling, we got back in touch with each other and arranged to meet up in her home city of Christchurch. As mentioned throughout this book, we spent some time together, became close friends and went on a road trip around the South Island with another sommelier friend called Keri. Nicki is the person featured in the photograph on the front cover of this book. I think that photo I took in 2009 of the iconic "Nin's Bin" Crayfish Shack entirely encapsulates our journey.

I later became aware, as she opened up to me, that she was an alcoholic. Whilst working in London, she got used to the usual rigmarole of long, unsociable hours, routinely going out after work and socialising with her work colleagues. This is quite typical behaviour, especially by those who work in bars and restaurants. But eventually everything takes its toll. She decided to take the courageous step to go back home, spend quality time with her family, get cleaned up and put herself through Alcoholics Anonymous. I admire her very much for her openness and honesty and the way she managed to turn her life around and get back onto the 'straight and narrow'. Nicki decided to change her career, as it was very important to get out of that 'all-consuming' lifestyle and environment. She put herself through college, met and settled down with a lovely guy and now works with kids. Nicki Mansfield is a wonderful person and is always in my thoughts positively reinforcing and reminding me that when you put your mind to it, you can certainly achieve anything.

"The sommelier ought to be seen as a positive force, almost as an interpreter and guide who can shepherd a meal along a rewarding and enlightening path. Yet too often the looming approach of the sommelier provokes the fight-or-flight instinct. Without thinking, consumers withdraw into a protective posture to ward off attacks on the wallet and other sensitive parts. Sommeliers can be your best friends. Allow yourself to trust them. They measure their success by your happiness. In fact, the greatest pleasure for most sommeliers is to watch you enjoy wines they love. Your job? Simply to be clear about your budget. No moment is more awkward for both sommeliers and consumers than discussing prices. No guests want to appear cheap, particularly in front of somebody — a date, a business acquaintance — they are trying to impress. But neither do they want to spend more than they can afford. Smart sommeliers have found ways to finesse the question. Sommeliers are wary of complete responsibility, like a cab driver you have directed to choose the fastest route."

Eric Asimov - Journalist, New York Times

ROVING SOMMELIER

"The roving sommelier is the facilitator of liquid enjoyment."

Over the years, almost like the legendary Bruce Forsyth with his now-iconic, comedic catchphrases, that has become a bit of a personal 'tagline'. Roving Sommelier is also the name of my business, which includes an independent wine consultancy, bespoke wine tours and networking opportunities, an events company that hosts pop ups, events, tastings and master classes, a wine merchant, tasting room, deli, gallery and store. Our aim is to bring you a wonderful selection of premium beverages, artisan produce and professional services and share some amazing experiences with food and wine. In addition, we like to make our activities fun and engaging and to branch out to a wider audience by using social media. Please visit our website at

www.rovingsommelier.com for further details.

However, I often ask myself how did I get to this stage and why did I call my business "Roving Sommelier"? My journey with 'roving sommelier' started a few years ago, probably on those first trips "Down Under" in 2001/02. Valuable time spent engaging with fellow sommeliers and meeting other people within the wine business and wine makers taught me a lot and I was inspired. As soon as I returned to London, I started to incorporate flights of wine tasters into my wine programme and to broaden the selection of the wines I served by the glass. This gave me a greater opportunity to engage with the customer, to introduce the wines that I had discovered, vineyards to which I had travelled and the wine makers I had met, but also enabled the diner an opportunity to try something new. For me, this is the most personally satisfying part of my profession. Hence, "the sommelier is the facilitator of liquid enjoyment" and 'roving sommelier' soon became my 'alter ego'.

Whilst I worked at Fifth Floor at Harvey Nichols (between 2003-2006), I approached Dominic Ford (Food and Beverage Retail Director) with a couple of ideas. First, to dedicate a small amount of space within the wine shop area towards an enomatic-style machine wine dispenser system. Here, it was my aim to enhance and maximise the opportunity to develop the accessibility of wine and offer to our customers sample tasters before they made their purchases. Unfortunately, my idea was not taken on board. As this was around 2003/4 it meant that this cutting-edge and innovative concept would have pre-dated the now-iconic "Wonder Bar" at Selfridge's and establishments such as The Sampler.

My second idea was for Harvey Nichols to take over the space on the second floor at Oxo Tower (it already ran a very successful restaurant operation on the 8th floor) and to convert it into a multi-purpose, tasting room and retail space. Here, there would also be plenty of room for sampling wine dispensers and hosting events, masterclasses and other wine and food activities. Once again, my idea was not taken on board. Perhaps the numbers didn't stack up? Maybe I am ahead of my time? Who knows...

During my time as a top flight wine buyer and head sommelier, one of the most pleasurable and rewarding parts of my job was to host regular wine tastings, master classes and events. For instance, whilst at Fifth Floor at Harvey Nichols, we hosted fabulous wine maker dinners and masterclasses, including a spectacular mixologist event in collaboration with New Zealand-based vodka company "42 Below". On Monday evenings, all wines were available in the restaurant at wine shop prices and this soon went down a storm with the regulars.

At Orrery I created a 'wine tasting club' from scratch, which consisted of many eager and regular clients and restaurant diners and hosted events with many Kiwi wine makers and wineries. Of course, my favourite was the Dog Point tasting, as I felt that the situation had come around full-circle. I hosted many regular wine tastings on the summer terrace too, weather-permitting, naturally.

It was whilst I was at Orrery (2006-2009) that I started blogging about food, wine and travel and then a regular wine column featured in the Marylebone Journal. You see, when you're a sommelier you have such a great opportunity to travel the world and visit the vineyards. My blog, which has now evolved into a proper website and social media resource first started out as a kind of diary and for me to record these activities. I always mentioned somewhere within my blog posts my 'alter ego' - roving sommelier and finished off with "the epicurean odyssey continues..." This eventually became my strap line and essence to my personal journey.

Later, after I had taken some time off during 2009 and on my return from New Zealand, I approached a couple of contacts. Inspired by the great 'head to head' blind tasting hosted a few years ago at The Groucho Club in London, where many Austrian wines successfully received world wide acclaim by 'beating' a selection of top class white Burgundies and other iconic wines, I had always wanted to inspire and galvanise people to come together and attend similar tastings. However, how was I going to do it, who should be the target market and what would be the theme of these blind tastings? This idea is not new, but I wanted to do something unique and memorable. I decided that for this one the theme would be Pinot Noir, as for most wine lovers it is clearly regarded as "The Holy Grail".

As a starting point for my roving sommelier pop up wine tastings, I decided to focus on the influential wine communicators, wine experts, bloggers and sommeliers within the wine industry. So, in January 2010 I spoke to Kate Sweet and Angela Reddin and told them my idea and plan to lay on such an event. They went away and put it together, as they had the experience and the contacts and during autumn 2010 "Pinot Puzzle" was hosted in London. It was fantastic and hats off to them for organising such a spectacle. They managed to get Helen Masters of Ata Rangi and Blair Walter and Nicola Greening of Felton Road involved to act as guest speakers too. For me, it was a great opportunity to do a bit of networking, consolidate all my ideas, and gather much exciting content and videos that could be uploaded onto my newly-launched website. On a personal note, this 'dummy run' was very valuable experience, but without taking any of the risk or expense and to clearly see what it took to run an event like this in the future. I decided that to focus on the grape variety for the theme would be the best way forwards and to host at least two blind tastings per year.

In March 2011, I hosted "Ravenous for Riesling" - a blind tasting of 75 Riesling wines from around the world.

In June 2011, I hosted "Craving for Chenin" - a blind tasting of 40 Chenin Blanc wines from around the world.

In March 2012, I hosted "Savouring for Syrah" - blind tasting of 65 Syrah/Shiraz wines from around the world.

In September 2013, I hosted "Grooving For Gruner" - a blind tasting of 40 Gruner Veltliners from around the world and a Pinot Noir tasting and dinner with Tim Kerruish, co-owner and wine maker at Folding Hill Vineyard in Central Otago.

My wine business consultancy, website and social media resource now includes an ecommerce platform with links to New Zealand vineyards, craft beer microbreweries, artisan cheesemongers, coffee roasters and wine tourism. As a business we also continue to collaborate with many interesting brands and artisan products and to develop and host engaging wine and food-based activities.

For further details, please go to www.rovingsommelier.com

Follow our tweets and updates on Twitter @rovingsommelier

Connect with us at our Official facebook page at
www.facebook.com/rovingsommelier

Over the years, you begin to realise that you're extremely fortunate to have the opportunity to meet so many wonderful people and travel to so many places. I really enjoy what I do as "The Roving Sommelier" and photography is an important part of the communication of my passion, enthusiasm and experience. I started getting into photography many years ago and it still remains one of my hobbies, even though everything is purely amateur. I like to use photos, and especially more so now, the medium of video (I have produced a few hundred via my Roving Sommelier You Tube channel since late 2010) to encapsulate and broadcast my experiences. Unfortunately, I lost many of my original photos and a few of them ended up on my Facebook profile (which is no longer active) and the more recent ones have been incorporated into various blog articles and calendars.

I've been very lucky to visit many vineyards and spend time with fabulous wine makers. With regards to my photography, my biggest inspiration have been Kevin Judd (of Cloudy Bay and Greywacke fame) and Michael Seresin, who I met many years ago. I am also inspired by Craig Potton, with whom I met up with in 2014 at his eponymous gallery in his native city of Nelson. I particularly enjoy taking photos of landscapes. New Zealand is a stunningly beautiful country and if you ever have the opportunity to visit, I hope you enjoy it as much as I do.

To take a look at Craig Potton's stunning work please click on his website at www.craigpottongallery.co.nz

RECIPE INDEX & WINES

RECIPES INSPIRED BY NORTHLAND

Smoked fish and avocado sandwich

—1 cup smoked fish, flaked
—1 shallot, finely chopped
—4 large artichoke hearts in oil, drained and chopped
—2 sticks celery heart, finely sliced
—2 teaspoons lemon zest
—2 tablespoons lemon juice
—Salt and freshly ground black pepper
—1/4 cup mayonnaise, preferably home-made
—1/4 cup flat-leafed parsley
—1 avocado, cut into chunks
—8 large slices sourdough bread

Combine the smoked fish with the shallot, artichoke hearts, celery, lemon zest and juice. Season well with salt and pepper and stir well. Gently fold through the mayonnaise then fold in the parsley and avocado. Spread this mixture on to 4 slices of the bread; you can butter the bread if you like but it is not necessary. Put the lids on, cut the sandwiches in half and serve.

A good bowl of olives on the side works well with these delicious sarnies.

Wine suggestion: 2010 Takatu Pinot Gris

Tuna steaks with Romesco-style sauce

For the sauce
—2 large tomatoes
—2 small red hot chillies
—2 large red peppers
—25g blanched almonds
—25g hazelnuts
—3 and a 1/2 tablespoons extra virgin olive oil (choose a mild

Spanish oil)
—1 slice day-old white toast bread
—2 large cloves garlic, crushed
—1 and a 1/2 teaspoons red wine vinegar
—Salt

—1 tablespoon olive oil
—1 tablespoon clarified butter
—4 small tuna steaks, cut 2-3cm thick
—Flour
—Salt and freshly ground black pepper

Put the tomatoes and chillies on an oven tray and grill under a high heat. Remove the chillies when they are charred but grill the tomatoes on both sides until the skin splits and blackens. Roughly chop the chillies, discarding seeds if preferred. Skin the tomatoes and chop the flesh, discarding seeds and cores. Grill the peppers until charred, cool, remove skin, cores and seeds and chop the flesh. Toast the nuts in a hot oven till lightly golden, about 7 minutes for the almonds and 10 minutes for the hazelnuts. Put the hazelnuts in an old cloth, form it into a bundle and rub off the skins. Heat 11/2 tablespoons of the oil in a small frying pan over a medium heat. Fry the bread till golden, then wipe out the pan and add the rest of the oil and the garlic. Cook gently until a pale golden colour. Put the nuts and fried bread (broken into pieces) into a food processor and tip in the garlic and all the oil. Process to a paste then add the peppers, chillies, tomatoes, salt and vinegar and process again till well blended. Turn into a bowl and serve; if not for immediate use, cover and chill (use within 24 hours).Heat a large heavy-based frying pan over a medium-high heat. When it is hot, add the oil, allow the oil to get hot, and then add the butter. Meanwhile, dust the tuna steaks with flour. Cook 11/2-2 minutes a side, depending on how rare you prefer it. Transfer to a heated serving dish, sprinkle with salt and pepper and serve immediately with the Romesco sauce.

Romesco sauce has many uses. In this thickened form, its

chunky texture, smoky resonance and finishing jab of acidity make a great counterpoint to the tuna steaks. Tuna changes its allegiance to wine, depending on what it is served with. In this combination, the sweet taste of red peppers and charred smoky flavours in the Romesco ensure a red wine with sweet fruit will make an enjoyable match.

Wine suggestion: 2009 Hyperion "Eros" Pinot Noir

RECIPES INSPIRED BY GREATER AUCKLAND

Warm pumpkin salad and Puhoi feta
—50q manuka woodchips
—Tinfoil
—250g button mushrooms
—1 medium pumpkin or squash, peeled and cut into large cubes
—100ml good quality extra virgin olive oil
—100g pumpkin seeds
—200g mesclun salad mix
—1 small red onion, thinly sliced
—3 tomatoes, quartered
—250g Puhoi feta cheese
—300g of your favourite salad dressing or vinaigrette

Place wood chips in a cup made of tinfoil in a frying pan. Lay out mushrooms on a wire rack over wood chips. Cover with another pan of equal size or pot lid, and smoke for 8-10 minutes over a medium heat. Turn off heat and leave mushrooms covered for another 5 minutes. Do this in a fish smoker if you have one.
Once cool, dice mushrooms into large pieces.

Boil pumpkin for 5 minutes or until it is half cooked. Put into an ovenproof dish along with olive oil and pumpkin seeds. Roast in a pre-heated oven at 200 degrees for 15 minutes or until cooked. After 10 minutes add the diced mushrooms.

In a large bowl toss salad greens, onion, tomatoes and feta together. Add pumpkin, mushrooms, seeds and olive oil to salad mix. Toss again and divide between salad bowls. Drizzle with your favourite dressing.

Wine suggestion: 2010 Coopers Creek, "The Little Rascal" Arneis

Parmesan Panna Cotta with braised figs and prosciutto

Please note: to get all recipes and wine pairings, please scan QR codes with your smartphone

Pearl barley risotto with butternut squash, pine nuts and goat's cheese

Pan-fried Hapuku

—6 medium tomatoes
—50ml extra virgin olive oil
—4 shallots, finely chopped
—4 sprigs thyme
—1 teaspoon crushed garlic
—Sea salt and freshly ground pepper
—6 Kalamata olives
—1 teaspoon sherry vinegar
—6 large potatoes, peeled and chopped
—20ml lemon juice
—2 teaspoons crushed garlic
—100ml extra virgin olive oil
—Salt and freshly ground pepper
—2 heads spinach, washed
—4 hapuku medallions (use monkfish as an alternative)

To cook the tomato salad, cut tomatoes in half and de-seed. Place in a single layer on an oiled tray with shallots, thyme and garlic. Season with sea salt and bake in the oven at 150 degrees until the skin starts peeling from tomatoes (about 5 minutes). Refresh and leave to cool after removing skins.

Drain oil from tomatoes and reserve. Roughly chop them with the olives and place in a bowl with the vinegar. Add reserved oil and keep at room temperature.

Boil potatoes until soft, drain well, mash, add lemon juice, garlic and oil and combine. Season and keep warm. Wilt spinach in a little butter, season and just before serving place on top of the mashed potato.

Sear hapuku fillets for one minute on each side. Transfer to a pre-heated oven for 5-7 minutes.

Wine suggestion: 2010 Goldwater Estate "Zell" Chardonnay

My spicy fish and seafood broth with noodles

—250g fresh prawns (I prefer to use Thai) or a mixture of different seafood (e.g prawns, mussels, calamari)
—Quarter medium onion, finely chopped
—2 cloves garlic, finely chopped
—One inch piece of fresh ginger, finely grated/chopped
—Half inch piece galangal (optional), finely grated/chopped
—One stick celery, finely chopped
—One stick lemongrass
—Pinch chilli
—2 teaspoons ground coriander
—Half teaspoon ground cumin
—3 Kaffir lime leaves (optional)
—Thai basil, (optional)
—One tablespoon Thai fish sauce (optional)
—Palm sugar (optional)
—Juice and zest one fresh lime
—Half litre chicken stock
—Half litre coconut milk
—200g rice noodles, fresh coriander roughly chopped

In a large pan, sweat off the onions, celery, garlic, ginger, galangal and spices, without colouring over a medium heat. Add the optional lime leaves and Thai basil. Carefully bash the lemongrass stalk to release its aromatic and citrus perfume. Add this to the pan so that its fragrance infuses into the other ingredients. Be careful though, because if you add too much lemongrass the dish will end up tasting like citrus toilet cleaner.

Now add the liquids – firstly the chicken stock and Thai fish sauce and let reduce a little by bringing the temperature up to a simmer. Again be careful, especially as sometimes it can be salty. Taste and adjust the seasoning if required. You can add the optional palm sugar at this stage to balance up the saltiness. Add the coconut milk and again reduce a bit. The broth will thicken a little.

Add the prawns/seafood and cook for a further two minutes.

Add the rice noodles, lime juice, zest and chopped coriander. I also like to add the aromatic roots, not only because I don't like to waste anything, but also because they add a lovely taste to the dish. Toss everything together, again check the seasoning to taste.

Serve in nice warm bowls and tuck in! You should end up with an authentic taste of the pan-Asian cuisine – hot, sour, salty and sweet all in perfect harmony.

Wine suggestion: 2010 Kumeu River "Coddington Vineyard" Chardonnay

A recipe from Enzo Bettio

To get recipe and wine pairing, please scan QR code with your smartphone

Medallions of Venison with kumara and apple rosti and black-currant jus

—50ml blackcurrant puree
—200ml venison jus or beef stock
—1 large kumara, grated
—Half apple, julienned
—1 egg
—Pinch of salt and freshly ground black pepper
—Half onion, diced
—200g baby spinach
—20g chopped garlic
—100ml cream
—Salt, pepper and nutmeg
—360g venison loin, cut into 4 medallions

To cook the jus, blend ingredients (blackcurrants and stock) and reduce for 10 minutes.

To cook the rosti, combine all the ingredients. Make small patties and fry in some clarified butter until golden brown. Set aside and keep warm.

To cook the spinach, fry onion, spinach and garlic in a little butter. Once spinach is wilted, add cream and seasonings. Reduce and keep warm.

Fry the venison medallions in very hot oil for 2-3 minutes on each side. Allow to rest.

To assemble, place the rosti on a warm plate, then place a venison medallion on rosti and top with spinach. Spoon jus around. Garnish with rosemary and blackberries.

Wine suggestion: 1998 Stonyridge Larose, Waiheke Island

RECIPES INSPIRED BY WAIKATO/BAY OF PLENTY

Flounder with beurre noisette and chips
—85g unsalted butter
—2 large flounders
—2 tablespoons plain flour
—Salt and freshly ground black pepper
—Half lemon, cut into wedges
—4 large potatoes, preferably King Edwards
—Vegetable or rapeseed oil for frying
—Salt

Ask your friendly fishmonger to cut off the heads, fins and tail. Place fish in flour in a large tray and season with salt and pepper.

Set a frying pan over a medium heat. Once hot, add some clarified butter. Quickly dip each fish into the seasoned flour and shake off excess. Immediately add the fish to the sizzling ho butter and fry for about 3-4 minutes on each side until golden brown and cooked through. Remove and keep warm on plates.

Place 30g cold butter in a small saucepan. Set over a medium heat until it turns golden brown and smells of hazelnuts. Immediately pour over the fish. Garnish with lemon and serve immediately with chips.

To make the chips, peel the potatoes and cut into thin chip-sized batons. Place in a large bowl of cold water and leave to soak for 30 minutes to remove the excess starch. Preheat the oil in a deep fat fryer to 150 degrees.

Drain the potatoes and pat dry on some paper towelling. Cook in batches so that the oil retains its temperature as the potatoes 'blanch'. Fry the potatoes until they have a crisp uncol-oured skin with a soft centre. This will take around 4 minutes. Remove from the oil and shake off the excess before spreading them out to cool on some kitchen paper.

Once cold, either set aside or, if you are preparing well ahead, chill until shortly before needed. The blanched chips should be at room temperature before the final cooking.

To serve, heat the oil to 180 degrees and cook the blanched chips in batches for about 3 minutes or until golden and crisp.

Drain on kitchen paper, tip into a bowl and salt liberally before dropping a pile of chips on each plate next to the fish.

Wine suggestion: 2010 Mystery Creek "Reserve Gold Medal Waikato" Chardonnay

Fresh pappardelle pasta with rabbit sauce

To get recipe and wine pairing, please scan QR code with your smartphone

Rib eye steak with grilled and marinated vegetables

—Rib eye steaks
—2 capsicums, cut into large slices
—3 courgettes, sliced
—2 tablespoons olive oil
—2 tablespoons balsamic vinegar
—3 golden kumara
—2 tablespoons butter
—Seasonings
—Beef stock red wine reduction

Clean and trim the steaks or alternatively ask your butcher to do for you. Char-grill capsicums and courgettes and marinate in oil and vinegar. Roast whole kumara, peel and mash with butter and seasonings. Reheat vegetables in the oven.

Sear steaks on a hot griddle pan and cook to required liking. Take off and leave to rest. De-glaze the pan with beef stock red wine reduction. Serve with veggies and kumara.

Wine suggestion: 2008 Mills Reef "Reserve" Merlot Malbec

Roast pheasant

To get recipe and wine pairing, please scan QR code with your smartphone

RECIPES INSPIRED BY GISBORNE

Seared tuna with chilli sesame dressing

To get recipe and wine pairings please scan QR code with your smartphone

Red curry mussels

—2 large onions, peeled and sliced
—1 teaspoon ground ginger
—4 cloves garlic, crushed
—1 tablespoon Thai red curry paste
—3 stalks lemongrass, bottom 10cm only, chopped
—300ml coconut cream
—250ml milk
—100ml cream
—2 tablespoons tomato puree
—48 mussels
—1 handful fresh coriander - you can use the stalks as well, as they provide much flavour.

In a large pot, cook the onions in a little oil without browning. Add ginger and garlic and cook for 2 minutes. Add red curry paste and cook for a further minute. Add all the other ingredients except mussels and coriander and cook until sauce thickens.

Add mussels and poach for 4-5 minutes. Garnish with fresh coriander and naan bread for dipping.

Wine suggestion: 2006 Vinoptima "Ormond" Gewurztraminer

For me, Gewurztraminer will always be the ultimate wine pairing for a spicy, aromatic dish such as this. However, please note that Vinoptima wines are made in very small quantities.

RECIPES INSPIRED BY HAWKE'S BAY

Smoked trout soufflé

—75g butter
—50g flour
—300ml milk
—5 egg yolks
—125g smoked trout fillets, mashed into a thick pureé
—Salt and pepper
—Pinch of thyme and nutmeg
—6 egg whites, beaten until stiff

Make a white sauce with the butter, flour and milk. When it has cooled, stir in the egg yolks and fish mixture. Add seasonings, thyme and nutmeg. Fold in the egg whites. Pour into a large buttered soufflé dish or individual ramekins. Pop into a preheated oven at Gas mark 6 (200 degrees) for 20 to 25 minutes, and do not open the oven door to take a peek during the cooking time. Serve immediately.

Wine suggestion: 2010 Bilancia Pinot Gris

Trout "en papillotte" with tartare sauce

Roast venison with kumara gratin

—4 x 140g venison fillets
—30g butter
—Salt and pepper
For the kumara gratin
—200ml milk
—300ml double cream
—1 sprig of thyme and rosemary
—4 garlic cloves
—4 large kumara, peeled
—Knob of butter
—Salt

Preheat the oven to 180. Put milk, cream and herbs into a saucepan. Infuse over a low heat for 20 minutes. Remove from heat, cover and allow to infuse for further 30 minutes. Strain the mix and discard herbs.

Using a mandolin or sharp knife, slice the kumara lengthways into 3mm slices. Line a small, deep casserole dish with soft butter and build the grating, seasoning each layer and pouring the infused cream mixture on top. Place in the oven for 50-60 minutes covered until cooked through. Remove the cover and bake for further 10 minutes. Allow to rest for at least 15 minutes before serving. Heat a frying pan on a medium heat. When smoking hot add butter, season venison well and colour on all sides. Place in oven for 2 minutes at 180 degrees Turn meat and cook for further 2 minutes. Remove and allow to rest for 10 minutes. Portion up kumara gratin, re-heat to temperature and place on plate. Slice the venison and place on top of the gratin. Add any cooking juices left from the meat to the dish.

Wine suggestion: 2004 Bilancia "La Collina" Syrah

Roast rack of lamb with kumara and sage mash

—4 small French-trimmed racks of lamb.
—1 kg kumara
—Half cup purple sage, chopped
—2 parsnips
—Half cup grain mustard
—1 cup dried cranberries
—1 cup beef stock
—Half cup redcurrant jelly
—Half cup red wine

To prepare the mash, peel the kumara and boil in lightly salted water until soft. Drain well, add sage and keep warm.

Peel parsnips and cut with potato peeler into long strips. Deep-fry or oven bake until crisp and set aside for garnish.

Sear racks of lamb in a hot, oiled pan, then spoon on mustard and dried cranberries to form a crust. Roast in preheated oven at 180-200 degrees for around 10 minutes. While meat is roasting, combine ingredients for jus and warm through.

To assemble, spoon kumara mash onto plates, cut each rack in half and link bones. Place standing up nicely on mash, drizzle jus over racks and top with crispy parsnip strips. Serve with seasonal vegetables

Wine suggestion: 1998 Te Mata "Awatea" Cabernet Merlot

RECIPES INSPIRED BY WAIRARAPA

Waikanae crab cakes

Wild mushroom risotto

To get recipes and wine pairings, please scan QR code with your smartphone

Spiced crab salad

—300g white crab meat
—2 limes
—1 small red Thai chilli
—Salt and freshly ground black pepper
—4 Little Gem lettuce hearts
—1 bunch watercress (trimmed and washed)
—1 tablespoon mint leaves (roughly chopped)
—A handful of coriander leaves
—4 spring onions (finely sliced)
—5 inner sticks celery (finely sliced)
—1 red pepper (quartered, deseeded and finely sliced)
—4 tablespoons extra virgin olive oil

Pick through the crab meat carefully. Gently squeeze out any excess moisture and place the meat in the bowl. Finely grate and juice one lime. Mix the zest and juice into the crab meat. Add the chilli and season to taste.

Wash the lettuce leaves and pat dry. Place the smaller leaves in a mixing bowl with the watercress sprigs, mint, coriander, spring onions, celery and red pepper.

When you are ready to serve, toss the watercress salad in 2 tablespoons of lime juice from the second lime and the extra virgin oilve oil. Season to taste and divide between 4 plates. Spoon the crab meat onto the 8 remaining lettuce leaves and serve 2 per portion.

Wine suggestion: 2010 Palliser Estate Riesling

Stir-fried scallops with vegetables

—16 Queen scallops, cleaned and trimmed
—6 spring onions, each cut into 4 long strips
—225g fresh bean sprouts
—2 large carrots, cut into long thin julienne strips

—Salt and pepper
—Vegetable oil for frying
—1 tablespoon dry sherry or rice wine
—Quarter teaspoon grated fresh ginger
—Quarter teaspoon finely chopped garlic
—1 teaspoon light soy sauce
—Pinch Chinese Five Spice Powder
—Juice of one lemon

Season the scallops with the salt and pepper and fry briskly for 2 minutes in 1 or 2 tablespoons in oil – use a wok if you have one, otherwise a frying pan will do. Add the sherry, soy sauce, lemon juice and allow to bubble for a minute. Tip onto a dish and keep warm.

Add more oil to wok if required. When very hot, add all the other ingredients and stir-fry over a fierce flame for 2-3 minutes. Return the scallops to the wok and whiz around a couple of time for no more than 20 seconds. Serve immediately with steaming boiled rice or noodles

Wine suggestion: 2009 Escarpment Pinot Blanc

Twice cooked pork belly

—1.5kg pork belly, skin on
—2 cups sea salt
—1 cup sugar
—1 heaped teaspoon smoked paprika
—Half cup oregano leaves
—Small bunch thyme
—2 onions, chopped
—2 carrots, peeled and chopped
—4 cloves garlic, peeled and halved

Score the skin of the pork. In a food processor blend the salt, sugar, paprika and herbs. Liberally rub the pork with the dry marinade, then place in the fridge overnight.

The following day, rinse the pork well then soak in several changes of cold water for 30 minutes. Pat dry and place skin side down in a roasting tin.

Preheat oven to 160 degrees. In a medium saucepan over a moderate heat, fry the onions, carrots and garlic in oil until well browned. Add the stock and bring to boil. Once boiling, pour over pork, cover roasting dish with tinfoil and braise for 3 ½ hours.

Remove the pork from the oven, uncover, tip off most of the stock, strain it and reserve. Place a heavy tray on top of the pork and a few weights to compress it. Refrigerate overnight. These two stages can be done days before the meal as the pork keeps well and matures in flavour.

Preheat oven to 180 degrees. Slice the pork into portions required (rectangles). In a small saucepan reheat stock. Crackle up the pork skin for about five minutes and ensure pork is cooked through and browned on each side. Serve with seasonal vegetables and potatoes or a hearty bean stew.

Wine suggestion: 2009 Urlar Pinot Noir

Beef Pesto (A 'classic' Sugar Club recipe from Peter Gordon)

"This was our hallmark dish at the Wellington Sugar Club, and now, twenty seven years later, it features on the menu at The Sugar Club in Auckland. I have no idea how I came up with the idea of marinating beef in soy and vinegar (it even sounds odd now I think about it), but people would come into the restaurant just to have it. When we first opened in London in 1995, we would get New Zealanders phoning up to ask if I was the same chef that had created Beef Pesto in Wellington, and would we please put it on the menu for their birthday, wedding, anniversary etc. It may sound a little odd, but then I'm told so much of my food is, but it really works. You could use ready-made pesto, or make your own from my recipe below." – Peter Gordon

—1 piece of mid beef fillet, trimmed, about 1.5kg
—500ml tamari, or soy sauce
—250ml cider vinegar
—1 red chilli, moderately hot
—12 cloves of garlic, peeled
—quarter cup seed mustard
—150ml cider vinegar
—half teaspoon salt
—half teaspoon cracked black pepper
—350ml olive oil
—half bunch silverbeet, about 400g, shredded finely, stems and all, and washed well to remove dirt
—3 zucchini, diced
—2 medium-sized raw beetroot, peeled and finely julienned
—1 cup basil pesto*

Marinate the beef at least two days in advance.

Put the tamari, the first amount of cider vinegar, the chilli and six cloves of the garlic into a blender and purée to a fine consistency for 30 seconds.

Lay the fillet in a long dish, just large enough to hold it, and pour the marinade over it, cover with clingfilm and place in the fridge. Every 12 hours, turn the beef over to expose all of it to the marinade. It can be left to marinate for up to 4 days.

Just before you cook the beef, take it out of the marinade and drain well, then dry with a cloth.

Cut it into 8 equal pieces and leave to sit until you're ready to cook it.

Put the remaining garlic, the seed mustard, the second amount of cider vinegar, salt, pepper and olive oil into a food processor, purée for 30 seconds and pour into a large bowl.

Bring a large pot of boiling salted water to the boil, add the silverbeet and stir well.

After 30 seconds, add the zucchini and stir, and after 1 minute drain it all through a colander. (The silver beet and zucchini can be steamed if you prefer.)

Tip the hot vegetables into the bowl with the garlic dressing and stir well, add the beetroot and stir that in, then leave the bowl in a warm place.

Heat up a skillet or a grill to a high heat. Lightly oil the fillet on the cut sides and, for the best flavour, grill for no more than 2 minutes on each side.

Divide the beetroot salad amongst 8 plates.

Lay a piece of cooked fillet on top, then drizzle with the pesto.

For the pesto

Enough for a good-sized jar of pesto
—10 cloves of garlic, peeled
—3 loosely packed cups of fresh basil leaves
—1 loosely packed cup of mint leaves
—1 cup of roughly chopped flat parsley
—500ml olive oil
—1 cup pine nuts, lightly toasted a golden brown and left to go cold
—1 cup finely grated Parmesan
—extra virgin olive oil

Put the garlic, herbs, olive oil and pine nuts into a food processor. Purée to a coarse paste, but be careful not to over work. Turn out into a mixing bowl and stir in the Parmesan. Stir in extra virgin olive oil to get the pesto to the consistency you want.

Wine suggestions: 2003 Craggy Range "Te Muna" Pinot Noir or 2009 Cambridge Road Syrah

"I cook with wine. Sometimes I even add it to food."
W.C Fields

Ox cheek braised in red wine (Recipe by Pierre Koffmann)

To get recipe and wine pairing, please scan QR code with your smartphone

Classic Kiwi Pavlova
—4 large egg whites at room temperature
—Pinch of salt
—1 cup, plus 2 tablespoons sugar, divided
—1 teaspoon distilled white vinegar
—1 teaspoon vanilla extract
—1 cup whipping cream
—3 cups sliced strawberries
—1 cup sliced peeled kiwi fruit

Preheat oven to 250°. Trace an 8 inch circle on a piece of parchment paper with a pencil. Place it pencil side down on a baking sheet. Put egg whites and salt in a large, very clean bowl. Beat with a handheld or stand mixer on high speed (preferably with whisk attachment) until foamy. Gradually add 1 cup sugar, a few tablespoons at a time, beating well after each addition, until stiff, shiny peaks form (4 to 5 minutes). Beat in vinegar and vanilla just until blended. Mound meringue onto traced circle on baking sheet, spreading to fill and mounding edges slightly higher than centre. Bake until meringue is firm and pale golden brown, about 1 ½ hours. Crack oven door and let pavlova cool completely, about 2 hours more. Carefully remove from baking sheet and transfer to a platter (it's normal for crust to crack a little). In a bowl, with a mixer on high speed, beat whipping cream just until soft peaks form. Turn mixer to low and beat in remaining 2 tablespoons sugar. Just before serving, top pavlova with whipped cream, strawberries, and sliced kiwi fruit. Cut into 8 wedges.

Wine suggestion: 2009 Escarpment "Hinemoa" Riesling

Selection of cheeses from Kapiti Cheeses

Wine suggestion: 2011 Urlar Pinot Gris, Walrarapa

RECIPES INSPIRED BY MARLBOROUGH

Crayfish in white wine

To get recipe and wine pairing, please scan QR code with your smartphone

Mussels with satay sauce

Thai fish cakes

To get recipes and wine pairings, please scan QR codes with your smartphone

A recipe for scallops from Jonas Karlsson

To get recipe and wine pairing, please scan QR code with your smartphone

Scallops ceviche

—Dozen scallops (hand-dived are the best)
—Juice of 3-4 limes
—1 fresh red chilli, finely chopped
—1 red onion, very thinly sliced
—2 spring onions, finely chopped
—1 clove garlic, finely chopped
—Sea salt and ground black pepper to taste

Take the fresh scallops and place them in a shallow dish. Pour over the marinade and leave for 3-4 hours in the fridge. Turn from time to time. And there you have it – serve up!

Wine suggestion: 2009 Framingham "Classic" Riesling or 2011 Yealands Estate "Reserve" Sauvignon Blanc

Green-lipped mussels

—24 whole shell mussels
—Olive oil
—1 tablespoon fresh herbs
—Quarter cup dry white wine
—1 teaspoon chopped fresh garlic
—Half teaspoon chopped red chilli

Heat a pot with a tight-fitting lid on full heat, add a few drops of olive oil and throw in the mussels. Sizzle for a few seconds, tossing around. Add all the other ingredients as quickly as possible and toss. Place lid on pot and give a good shake. Leave for 5-6 minutes without lifting lid. Open lid and check mussels are cooked (shells would have opened). If not, cook for a further minute. Serve in bowls and pour on some of the cooking liquor/broth. Garnish with chopped flat leaf parsley or coriander and squeeze of lemon. Please note – great big hunks of crusty bread are required for this dish!

Wine suggestion: 2011 Dog Point Vineyard Sauvignon Blanc

Seafood risotto

—Use whichever type of seafood is your favourite – mussels, squid, crayfish, prawns, crab etc
—One small onion, peeled and finely diced
—4 cloves garlic, finely chopped
—1 ½ tablespoons olive oil
—1 tablespoon butter
—Glass dry white wine
—10 cherry tomatoes, sliced
—200g Arborio rice
—1 litre fish or chicken stock infused with lemon and saffron
—Pinch chilli flakes (optional)
—Flat leaf parsley, finely chopped

Over a moderate heat, sweat onion and garlic in the olive oil and butter until they are just translucent without colour. Add Arborio rice and toast in pan for 1-2 minutes, stirring continuously. Add glass of wine and let bubble and evaporate, stirring continuously. Add a small pinch of chilli flakes and the chopped cherry tomatoes. Add saffron and lemon infused stock little by little, stirring continuously until rice is al dente. Add the seafood mix 2-3 minutes before the end of cooking time. There is nothing worse than over cooked and rubbery seafood.

To finish – squeeze some fresh lemon and garnish with finely chopped flat leaf parsley.

Wine suggestion: 2009 Te Whare Ra "Toru" or 2011 Lawson's Dry Hills Gewurztraminer

A simple recipe for gravadlax

—900g – 1.4kg middle-cut fresh salmon, boned and cut into two
  lengthways.
—A big handful of fresh dill.
—4 tablespoons coarse sea salt
—2 tablespoons caster sugar
—2 tablespoon crushed black peppercorns

Lay one fillet, skin down, in a non-metal dish. Cover with the dill, salt, sugar and black pepper. Lay the remaining salmon fillet, skin up, on top. Find a piece of hardboard a little larger than the fish, cover it with aluminium foil and place it, well weighted on the fish. Stand in the fridge for at least 72 hours. Turn it every 12 hours: every time you turn it, spoon the juices that have oozed out over the fish as if you were basting a turkey.

To serve – slice gravadlax in generously and garnish with cucumber and lemon. A touch of crème fraiche with a dash of fresh horseradish is also a nice accompaniment.

Wine suggestion: 2002 Fromm La Strada Chardonnay

Seafood, shellfish and fish platter

Basically, cook this array of your favourite seafood, shellfish and salmon any which way you wish. However, please do not skimp on the quality. Try to get the best, freshest fish you can find from your fishmonger. This is a real showcase for a delightful selection and you will need a stunning wine with the 'wow factor' to match.

Wine recommendation: 2009 Dog Point Vineyard "Section 94" or 2009 Astrolabe "Taihoa" Sauvignon Blanc

Asparagus with almonds (Recipe by Jess Latchford of Secrett's Direct)

—1kg English asparagus
—¼ cup butter
—¼ cup slivered almonds
—1 tablespoon fresh lemon juice
—½ teaspoon salt
—¼ teaspoon black pepper

Bring a large pot of salted water to a boil. Add asparagus and cook until colour turns bright green, 2 to 3 minutes. Remove, rinse under cold water, and drain. Set aside.

Melt butter in a small saucepan over medium heat. Add almonds and cook until lightly browned and fragrant, about 5 minutes. Add lemon juice and cook until liquid reduces and becomes cohesive, 1 to 2 minutes. Season with salt and pepper and pour over reserved asparagus. Serve immediately.

Wine recommendation: 2011 Isabel Estate Sauvignon Blanc

Butternut squash soup

A pair of Little Beauties

To get recipes and wine pairings, please scan QR codes with your smartphone

Perfect wine for a Friday fish supper

Cod loins, cabbage, peas and samphire

Savoy rack of lamb, golden kumara, braised Savoy cabbage, pea and mint salsa (Recipe by Chris Fortune)

Pot roast lamb

To get recipes and wine pairings, please scan QR codes with your smartphone

RECIPES INSPIRED BY NELSON

Simple pad thai supper

—1 pack dry rice noodles
—2 small packs fresh bean sprouts
—1 cup ground roast peanuts
—1 carrot, finely shaved
—Spring onion, finely shaved
—3 tablespoons cooking oil
—1 chicken breast or 12 prawns, shelled
—Lardons of bacon
—2 eggs
   500ml tamarind juice
—4 tablespoons nam pla (Thai Fish Sauce)
—6 tablespoons sugar
—3 tablespoons chilli sauce

Soak noodles in water for 3 hours. Mix the tamarind juice, fish sauce, sugar and chilli sauce in a small pan and stir well. Bring to the boil and simmer for 15 minutes.

Heat the cooking oil in wok or large frying pan until hot. Add the chicken or prawns and lardoons of bacon and stir until cooked. Add egg and stir in, then add the noodles and stir in well until cooked. Add pad thai sauce, ground roast peanuts and carrot and stir well, then add one pack of bean sprouts and the spring onion. When cooked place in bowls.

Squeeze on some lemon and serve with remaining bean sprouts.

Wine recommendation: 2011 Seifried Gruner Veltliner

Sautéed Whitebait (from the legendary Mokihinui River)

—250g whitebait
—Salt and freshly ground black pepper
—Mesclun salad mix
—Vinaigrette dressing
—Oil for frying

Now time for some cheffy-style pan shaking. Place a pan on high heat and add a touch of oil. When it starts to smoke, season whitebait with salt and pepper and place in pan, tossing until cooked, which will take around 40 seconds.

Toss mixed salad leaves in dressing and arrange on plate. Place hot whitebait on top and munch away happily with a fork. This will make an ideal snack in between wine tasting or quick supper.

Wine suggestion: 2010 Greenhough "Apple Valley" Riesling or 2009 Waimea Dry Riesling

Whitebait beignets (from the rugged West Coast)

—500g whitebait, washed and well-drained.
—225ml water
—90g butter
—125g flour
—3 eggs, lightly beaten
—1 teaspoon salt
—Generous grind of black pepper
—2 additional egg whites
—Oil to deep-fry

Put the water and butter into a saucepan. Melt butter, then bring to boil. Throw in sifted flour and stir vigorously until smooth making a roux. Cook for a further 2 minutes, so it does not catch.

Cool mixture. Beat in eggs one at a time and make something that resembles choux pastry. Add whitebait, salt and pepper, then fold in additional beaten egg whites to lighten the mixture.

Deep-fry spoonfuls of whitebait batter hot oil to make delicious and crispy beignets until golden and crisp. Drain thoroughly on kitchen paper. Serve with a wedge of lemon on side.

My suggestion would be to enjoy these with my two favourite Kiwi beers – Mac's Gold from Nelson or Monteith's Golden Lager from Greymouth. Choice!

Caper-crusted salmon

—4 x 250g – 300g portions of hot smoked salmon fillets, skin on and boned
—1 ½ cups capers, drained and squeezed dry
—¾ cup fresh parmesan, grated
—Zest of small 4 limes

To make crust, blitz drained capers in a food processor until finely chopped but not pulverised. Add parmesan and lime zest and mix through. Lay salmon portions on oven tray. Pile crust on top and spread over evenly.

Heat grill and place salmon under grill until crust starts to go crispy and salmon is warmed through (about 4-5 minutes). Be careful not to overcook the salmon, as you still need it to be moist. Serve with tossed rocket and watercress salad and a squeeze of lime.

Wine suggestion: 2005 Neudorf "Moutere" Chardonnay - (if you can still find it!)

AN EPICUREAN ODYSSEY

Duck salad with stone fruits

To get recipe and wine pairing, please scan QR code with your smartphone

RECIPES INSPIRED BY OTAGO

Goats' cheese fritters with watercress pesto

—2 tablespoons plain flour
—2 eggs, beaten
—75g fresh breadcrumbs
—25g ground hazelnuts
—8 slices of goats' cheese (preferably use Whitestone Dairy from Oamaru)
—50g watercress
—Half lemon, zest and juice
—50ml olive oil
—5 tablespoons water
—Sea salt and freshly ground black pepper

Place the flour egg and breadcrumbs on 3 plates. Mix the hazelnuts in with the breadcrumbs. Dust the cheese rounds in the flour, coat in beaten egg, then press into the breadcrumbs. Do this process for a second time, so that the cheese gets a double coating of breadcrumbs. Set aside.

To make the pesto, coarsely chop the watercress, then mix together with the lemon, olive oil and water. Generously season.

Heat the oil in a small enough pan to give you around a 6-8cm depth. Check the temperature by dropping a little piece of bread. It should sizzle nicely. Gently lower the breadcrumbed cheeses into the hot oil, two or three at a time. Cook until golden, which should take around 2-3 minutes. Place on some kitchen paper to drain and keep warm while you cook the rest. When ready to serve, drizzle with pesto.

Wine suggestion: 2010 Michelle Richardson Pinot Gris

Roast pork with crackling

—2.5kg shoulder of free range pork
—Sea salt
—Thyme
—4 onions
—Olive oil

Place the peeled, thickly-cut onions in the roasting tray with the thyme. This will add some flavour to the gravy and you will enjoy the tender onions with the meat.

Preheat the oven to 180 degrees. Sprinkle the pork skin with sea salt to aid crackling. Cook for just under 2 hours. At the end, turn up the heat to 200 degrees for final crisping of the skin for about 20 minutes. Rest the meat for a further 20 minutes before carving. Serve with lashings of apple sauce and all the trimmings.

Wine suggestion: 2011 Mt Difficulty Pinot Gris or 2009 Felton Road Chardonnay

Duck breasts with Szechuan pepper and cherries

Pork belly with fennel seed (Recipe sent in by Jo Mills of Rippon Vineyard)

To get recipes and wine pairings, please scan QR codes with your smartphone

Rabbit stew with artichokes

—1 rabbit cut into pieces
—1 bottle dry white wine
—100g carrots, sliced
—100g onions, sliced
—3 garlic cloves, chopped
—1 bouquet garni
—100g duck fat
—20 button onions, peeled
—50g chorizo, chopped
—25g plain flour
—4 large globe artichokes, trimmed, cleaned and cut into 6 pieces
—Salt and freshly ground pepper

First, ensure someone clever catches that pesky wabbit and shoots it. In a bowl, place the rabbit to marinade for 12 hours with the vegetables, wine and bouquet garni.

After 12 hours, drain the marinated rabbit and apt dry. Heat the duck fat in a large shallow pan, put in the rabbit pieces and seal on all sides. Add the onions and chorizo, and cook over a medium heat for 5 minutes, then sprinkle on the flour and cook for a few seconds. Strain the wine from the marinade into the pan, add the artichokes, season, cover and cook for about 30 minutes, until the rabbit and artichokes are tender. Serve up on nice warm plates with potatoes.

Wine suggestion: Amisfield, Bald Hills or Carrick Pinot Noir

Selection of cheeses from Whitestone Dairies

Wine suggestion: 2010 Pasquale Pinot Gris, Waitaki Valley

Venison in red wine with pancetta, wild mushrooms and Bluff oysters

—750g venison, cut into cubes
—1 tablespoon oil
—20 small shallots, peeled
—100g pancetta, cubed
—3 cloves garlic, peeled and chopped
—300ml red wine plus a tablespoon extra
—150g mushrooms
—10g wild mushrooms
—3 bay leaves
—700ml stock
—2 teaspoons cornflour
—12 Bluff oysters

Heat the olive oil in a large pan along with the shallots and cook them until golden. Add the pancetta and garlic and continue cooking for 5 minutes.

Remove everything from the pan, turn up the heat and add the venison. Brown the meat, then return the onions, pancetta and garlic to the pan. Our in the 300ml red wine and let it bubble for a few minutes, scraping the bottom of the pan to release any caramelised juices. Add mushrooms, bay and stock then season generously and bring up to the boil. Cover then simmer over a very low heat for 2.5 hours. Alternatively, transfer to the oven preheated to 160 degrees.

When the meat is tender, mix together the cornflour and red wine. Pour into the stew and bubble for a couple of minutes. Shuck the oysters, keeping all of the liquid. Drop the oysters with their juice into the stew and cook for about 5 minutes. Serve with some creamy mash and seasonal greens e.g curly kale or purple sprouting broccoli.

Wine suggestion: 2007 Mt Difficulty "Pipeclay Terrace" Pinot Noir

A tasty recipe for venison (Luke Mackay - freelance chef and Borough Market food blogger)

RECIPES INSPIRED BY CANTERBURY

Whitebait fritters (Mansfields of Merrivale style)

—125g fresh whitebait per portion
—1 egg
—Seasoning (salt and pepper)
—Butter
—Flour (optional)

Lightly beat the egg. Some recipes suggest separating the egg yolk and white so that when you whisk the egg whites they soufflé when the fritter is cooked. Mix in the whitebait. It is optional also to lightly coat them in flour first. Season the mix with salt and pepper. Pour whitebait batter mix into hot buttered frying pan. Cook whitebait patty until golden brown on each side. Serve and eat immediately, preferably with white bread and butter.

Wine suggestion: 2009 Black Estate Riesling

AN EPICUREAN ODYSSEY

Akaroa salmon tartare

Baked Canterbury Ostrich

To get recipes and wine pairings, please scan QR codes with your smartphone

The Perfect Roast Leg of Lamb

—1 leg of fresh lamb
—6-8 cloves of garlic
—4-5 10cm sprigs of fresh rosemary
—3 tablespoons extra virgin olive oil
—1 tablespoon Maldon salt
—Freshly ground black pepper
—A selection of vegetables such as kumara, potatoes, peppers, fennel bulbs, carrots, parsnips and garlic bulbs

Heat the oven to 200 degrees. Carefully trim as much of the surface fat and skin from the leg of lamb as you can. Peel the garlic cloves, cut each in half lengthwise and push into small incisions all over the lamb. Rub the surface of the leg with the oil. Chop the rosemary finely and scatter this over the lamb, on all sides. Also add the salt and pepper. Place the leg in a roasting pan, so that it fits snugly, and put in the heated oven. Cook for about one and a half hours and then rest for 10-15 minutes, covered with foil, while you make the gravy.

To roast the vegetables, heat the oil in a roasting pan, place the peeled and prepared vegetables in the oil, scatter with salt and pepper, and cook alongside the meat for 1 hour. To make the gravy, pour off any excess fat from the pan, leaving at least 2 table-spoons. Place the pan on a hot element, bring up to a medium to high temperature and stir in the flour. As the flour is absorbed into the fat, use a metal spoon to release the crusty meat juices that have formed on pan and stir in well. Add at least half the stock and stir continually, gathering up all the flavouring juices and meaty residue. As the gravy comes to the boil, turn the heat down to a gentle simmer and stir occasionally. Serve with gravy.

Wine suggestion: 2001 Pegasus Bay "Prima Donna" Pinot Noir

Selection of cheeses from Barrys Bay Cheese Farm on Banks Peninsula

Wine suggestion: 2008 Muddy Water "James Hardwicke" Riesling or 2009 Pegasus Bay "Encore" Riesling

I'm a passionate believer that white wines, in particular 'off-dry' Rieslings and other aromatic varietals are the perfect match for a selection of top-notch, artisan cheeses. For me, it's all in the acidity and balance between sweet and salty flavours. Try it for yourself!

RECIPES FROM ANNA HANSEN OF THE MODERN PANTRY

Anna has very kindly given me a couple of recipes which you may wish to try.

Grilled tamarind miso marinated onglet steak, turmeric and curry leaf besan chips

To get recipe and wine pairing, please scan QR code with your smartphone

Atari Goma panna cotta, saffron poached rhubarb, pistachio praline

Will make ten 275ml dariole moulds

For the rhubarb
—6 stalks rhubarb
—Pinch of saffron
—Juice of one orange
—Zest of ½ orange
—80g sugar

For the pistachio praline:
—½ cup pistachios, lightly toasted
—½ cup sugar
—Pinch of Maldon sea salt

For the panna cotta:
—800ml milk
—800ml double cream
—120g caster sugar
—5 leaves gelatine
—130g Atari Goma (Japanese tahini)

For the rhubarb: wash and cut into 2 inch lengths. Place in a pot and cook until tender.

For the praline: make a dry caramel with the sugar. Add the nuts and salt. Spread on a parchment paper-lined tray to cool. When cool smash into small pieces using a rolling pin or food processor. Store praline in an airtight container until ready to use.

For the panna cotta: Bring the milk, cream and sugar to boil and take off the heat. Soften the gelatine leaves in a bowl of cold water. When the milk has cooled slightly, add the gelatine and stir to dissolve then whisk in the Atari goma. Allow this mixture to become completely cool then pour into the moulds. Place them into the fridge and leave to set. Minimum of 3 hours.

To serve, quickly dip the moulds in a bowl of warm water to loosen the panna cotta and invert on a plate. Spoon on some of the rhubarb and scatter with the pistachio praline.

Wine suggestion: 2008 Pegasus Bay "Finale" Noble Chardonnay

Another tasty recipe from Anna Hansen

To get recipe and wine pairing, please scan QR code with your smartphone

My version of Asian-inspired coconut rice pudding

—100g short grain pudding rice
—1 can coconut milk
—500ml semi-skimmed milk
—200ml pineapple juice
—1 vanilla pod, scrape out seeds and include in mix with the pod
—3 cardamom pods, lightly-crushed
—1 teaspoon vanilla extract
—Zest of one lime
—A ripe large fresh mango (try to get Alphonso when in season)

Quite simple really – place all the ingredients, except the mango into a large saucepan. Cook gently over a low heat for about one hour, stirring occasionally. Be careful to check the rice every now and again and stir so that it doesn't stick. After a while the rice will cook and soften and absorb a lot of the liquid. It will also thicken as it cooks. I normally don't add any sugar, as I think the natural sweetness of the ingredients is sufficient. The lime zest also adds some fresh, fragrant citrus flavour, which not only works well with the coconut and mango, but also cuts through the richness. However, check to see if it suits your taste. Serve in bowls and mix in the chopped up chunks of juicy mango

Wine suggestion: Hunter's "Miru Miru" Methode Traditionelle, Marlborough. Alternatively, if you would prefer more of a conventional wine (more sweet), then I would recommend the 2006 Isabel Estate "Noble Sauvage", Marlborough. I have very fond memories of the 2006 vintage (I spent time during vintage with the Tiller family at Isabel Estate). The late-harvested Sauvignon Blanc grapes for this wine were picked on my birthday!

Rhubarb frangipane tart (a variation on classic Bakewell)

—375g pack Shortcrust Pastry
—4 medium eggs
—½ teaspoon ground cinnamon
—225g caster sugar, plus 4 tablespoons
—250g unsalted butter, softened
—300g ground almonds
—1 teaspoon almond extract
 —900g English rhubarb
—5 tablespoons strawberry jam
—25g toasted flaked almonds

Preheat the oven to 200°C, gas mark 6 and place a baking sheet in the centre of the oven to heat. Roll out the pastry to a 30cm round. Fold the top half of the pastry over the rolling pin then lift it onto a 27cm loose-bottomed flan tin, about 3cm deep. Using your hands, gently unfold the pastry and ease it down into the sides of the tin. Leave the excess pastry hanging over the edge and chill for 10 minutes. Trim off the excess pastry with a knife or roll the rolling pin over the top.

Prick the base of the pastry several times with a fork. Then lightly beat 1 egg and brush over the pastry case. Mix the cinnamon with 2 tablespoons of sugar and sprinkle evenly over the pastry.

Using an electric hand whisk, beat together 225g sugar with the remaining eggs, the butter, ground almonds and almond extract to make a thick paste. Spoon into the pastry case, spreading it to the edges

Bake on the preheated tray for 30 minutes until the filling is golden and feels just firm. Meanwhile, trim the rhubarb and cut into 2cm chunks. Place in a medium pan with the remaining 2 tablespoons sugar and 1 tablespoon cold water. Cover and cook over a low heat for 5-6 minutes until the rhubarb is just tender. Using a slotted spoon, arrange the rhubarb on the tart, piling it up in the centre and reserving the juices in the pan. Press the strawberry spread through a sieve and stir into the pan juices. Brush over the rhubarb to glaze. Scatter with the almonds and serve warm or cold with pouring cream.

Wine suggestion: 2008 Craggy Range "Fletcher Family" Noble Riesling, Marlborough

Duck rillettes (Misha's favourite)

—1 kg duck
—750g duck or goose fat
—75g salt
—15g pepper

Put the meat and fat into a heavy pan and cook gently for about 4 hours. When the pieces of meat are very well cooked, but not burned or brown, pour off the fat and reserve. Shred the meat using a couple of forks: do not use a food processor because it turns the meat into a paste and this is not the requited texture for a rillette. Add the seasoning. Put the shredded meat into glass jars and allow to cool.

Melt the reserved fat and cover the meat with it. Cool again. Seal the jars and store in a cool place.

Serve with toasted country bread and cornichons (gherkins). Even better still enjoy the rillette with pickled cherries, which combine excellently with the flavour of the duck.

Wine suggestion: 2009 Misha's Vineyard "High Note" Pinot Noir, Central Otago. However, if you have a preference for a white wine then the 2010 Misha's Vineyard "The Gallery" Gewurztraminer would be an exquisite combination.

Here is a recipe inspired by that indulgent evening on the Cloudy Bay Chef's Table at The Montagu and Carlos Teixeira's exquisite culinary skills:

Roasted foie gras with apple and truffle

To get recipe and wine pairing, please scan QR code with your smartphone

RECIPE FROM CRISTIAN HOSSACK (a.k.a "Crisso")

Pressed ham hock and water chestnut terrine with wok-fried mange tout, green mango and pickled bean-sprouts and pineapple sweet and sour dressing

To get recipe and wine pairing, please scan QR code with your smartphone

Seared salmon with noodle salad and soy-lime dressing

—150g salmon steak(s)
—10g piece fresh ginger
—300g soba noodles
—Bunch fresh coriander
—2 limes
—100ml soy sauce
—10g caster sugar
—50ml peanut oil
—2 cloves garlic
—1 whole red chilli
—1 bunch spring onion

Bring a large pan of salted water to the boil. Add the noodles and cook for 3 minutes. Drain and wash under cold water.

Chop the coriander leaves, ginger, chilli and garlic. Finely slice the spring onions. Heat a frying pan and add a little oil. Place the salmon in the pan and cook for a couple of minutes on each side. Remove from the pan.

For the dressing: Zest and juice the lime. Mix the soy sauce, coriander, ginger, chilli, garlic, peanut oil and sugar with the lime zest and juice. Add the dressing to the noodles and stir through the spring onions. Plate the noodles and place the salmon on top. Finish with a final drizzle of the soy-lime dressing.

Wine suggestion: 2010 Little Beauty "Black Edition" Pinot Gris, Marlborough

Spiced braised belly pork recipe (courtesy of wine consultant Angela Mount)

—1½ kg pork belly (skin removed and most of the fat removed then rolled and tied)
—Vegetable oil
—1 onion, chopped
—1 carrot, chopped
—1 celery stick, chopped
—5 cloves garlic, bashed
—50ml sherry vinegar
—50ml rice wine vinegar
—150ml soy sauce
—50ml mirin
—50ml saké
—8 star anise
—2 tablespoons coriander seeds
—1 tablespoons whole black peppercorns
—2 large red dried chillies
—1 cinnamon stick
—1 litre chicken stock

Heat 50ml oil in a heavy ovenproof casserole with a lid. Season the belly and then brown on all sides in the dish. Lift the meat out of the pan. Add the vegetables and garlic to the pan and cook for 5-10 minutes then add the vinegars, soy, mirin and sake. Cook for a further 10-15 minutes. Return the pork to the dish and add the stock and the remaining ingredients. Simmer with the lid on for 3-31/2 hours. Remove the meat; pass the cooking liquor through a sieve into a separate pan. Reduce the liquid by 2/3 to make a thin sauce. Slice the belly and serve with the sauce, steamed rice and broccoli fried with garlic and ginger

Wine suggestion: 2007 "John Forrest Collection" The White – 'multi-regional, multi-varietal blend'

RECIPES FROM PETER GORDON OF THE PROVIDORES

Galangal and smoked chicken laksa with soba noodles and a prawn

—15ml (1 Tablespoon) sunflower oil
—1 large roughly sliced red onion (don't peel it – the skin adds colour to the broth)
—100g sliced unpeeled galangal roots
—50g sliced fresh ginger
—1 hot-ish red chilli, sliced
—10g gapi (blachan or Thai shrimp paste)
—30g curry paste
—2 stems lemon grass, bash it with a meat hammer then roughly chop it
—10 kaffir lime leaves
—30g palm sugar
—30ml nam pla (Thai fish sauce)
—2 smoked chicken legs and thighs
—6 cloves smoked garlic
—50g tamarind paste
—800ml unsweetened coconut milk

—1 litre chicken stock

—100g soba noodles (made from buckwheat)

—12-16 peeled uncooked prawn tails, de-veined (allow 2 per portion)

—15ml sesame oil

—1/2 bunch coriander, leaves picked and chopped

—2 spring onions, thinly sliced

—Small handful crispy shallots

Heat the oil in a large pan until smoking, and then add the onion, galangal, ginger and chilli. Stir slowly but constantly to colour and wilt. Crumble the gapi into the pan and stir it in for a minute. Add the curry paste and cook another minute till aromatic, then add the lemongrass, lime leaves, palm sugar and nam pla and bring to a bubbly boil Stir in the chicken and smoked garlic then add the tamarind, coconut milk and chicken stock and bring to the boil. Turn to a simmer and leave cooking for 1 ½ hours. Give it a good stir, then pour through a fine chinoise (sieve) into a clean pot, pushing out as much liquid as you can. Leave to settle for a few minutes then skim the surface, and bring back to a simmer. Season it with extra fish sauce or salt, add lime juice to give it freshness then keep warm. Boil the noodles in a large pot of boiling water until al dente. A trick to help them cook properly is to add a cup of cold water each time they come to the boil it's called 'shocking the noodles' and helps buckwheat based noodles cook more evenly. Drain into a colander and keep covered.

Slice the prawn tails in half lengthways and toss with the sesame oil. Heat up a large pan or wok until fiercely hot then toss in the prawns and cook for just 30 seconds, stirring as they cook. Tip onto a warm plate. Heat up 6-8 serving bowls and divide the noodles amongst them. Ladle on the laksa broth then add the prawns. Garnish with the coriander, spring onions and crispy shallots.

Wine Suggestion: 2009 Pegasus Bay "Bel Canto" Riesling, Waipara

Crispy pork belly salad with tamarind chilli dressing

For the vegetable component of this salad I use a mixture of equal quantities of green papaya, green mango, jicama (yam bean) and carrots, all finely julienned. If some of those are hard to locate then you can replace with julienned carrots and cucumber and blanched bean sprouts.

For the belly, we brine it, after scoring, for 36 hours. It's then placed in a roasting dish sitting atop thick slices of potato and carrot and we tuck in red chillies, sliced ginger and lemongrass for extra flavour. Roast at 160ºC for 3 hours, at which point it'll be crisped up and cooked. You can eat it at this point, or press it for later. Take from the dish and lay in another flat dish on baking parchment. Lay more parchment on top and sit a kilogram or more of weight on top to press it. Leave to cool then place in the fridge. At this point you can either cut into large chunks and roast in the oven, or do as I do here and slice into 1cm thick pieces and deep-fry till crispy – delicious. The pork belly can also be replaced with a seared scallop.

—500g pork belly as described above cut into 1cm x 3cm pieces
—Oil for deep-frying
—2 Tablespoons tamarind paste
—½ red chilli, chopped (more or less to taste)
—2 Tablespoons grated pale palm sugar
—3 Tablespoons (45ml) lime juice
—Finely grated zest of 1 lime
—1 Tablespoon sesame oil
—2 Tablespoons vegetable oil
—2 Tablespoons soy sauce
—2 large handfuls of mixed julienned green mango, green papaya, jicama and carrots
—Small handful coriander on the stem, cut into 1cm pieces, use the stem too
—12 mint leaves, coarsely shredded

—6 basil leaves, shredded

—6 shiso leaves, shredded (or use extra basil and coriander)

—3 spring onions, sliced thin

—1 Tablespoon toasted sesame seeds

Heat the deep-fryer to 180ºC and cook the pork belly in batches don't overcrowd the fryer as it will splatter a bit. The belly is ready when crisp, drain well on kitchen paper.

In a small bowl whisk the tamarind, chilli and palm sugar together until the sugar has dissolved. Whisk in the lime juice and zest until combined, then whisk in the oils and soy sauce and taste for seasoning. It should be sweet and sour, rich and a little salty add more of the ingredients to your taste. In a large bowl toss everything else with a quarter of the dressing and divide amongst 6 bowls. Lay the cooked belly on top and drizzle with the remaining dressing.

Wine Suggestion: 2009 Seresin "Chiaroscuro", Marlborough. If you can't get hold of it, then I would suggest you try their Viognier.

Lime leaf-wrapped duck fritters with beetroot pesto

To get recipe and wine pairing, please scan QR code with your smartphone

Roast New Zealand venison loin with salsify and pickled plums

In New Zealand there are many deer farms breeding stock whose ancestors were running wild through our bush only 50 or so years previously. The white settlers from Scotland and England had brought the beasts out for weekend sport – and unfortunately they wreaked havoc as there are no predators in New Zealand to keep them at sustainable levels. The meat is tender, lean and healthy and available all year round unlike wild deer.

Pickle the plums at least 10 days before using to allow their flavour to develop and cure. The recipe here makes far more than you'll need, but they keep in the fridge for 2 months so long as they're kept covered with pickling liquid.

Salsify is a root vegetable used much like new potatoes in countries such as Belgium, Holland and parts of France. Rinse it well (it always comes covered with very fine sand) then peel using gloves (it's sticky), cut into 6cm lengths and place in acidulated water to prevent it discolouring.

—1kg ripe firm plums, wiped, cut in half and the stone removed
—1 vanilla bean, split lengthways and cut into 6
—½ red chilli
—100g peeled ginger root, thinly sliced
—6 star anise
—1 cinnamon quill (10-15cm)
—200g unrefined caster sugar
—400ml cider vinegar
—1kg trimmed New Zealand venison loin
—2 teaspoons dried wild oregano (from Greece and Turkey)
—2 Tablespoons extra virgin olive oil
—2 Tablespoons flour
—1 teaspoon turmeric
—600g peeled salsify, as described above
—1 Tablespoon fresh rosemary leaves
—½ lemon, sliced thin
—60g butter

—60g grated Parmigiano Reggiano
—Jus (reduced meat stock) to garnish, simmering
—Cress or micro greens to garnish

Heat up a 1.5 litre bottling jar by filling with very hot water. Place the vanilla, chilli, ginger, star anise, cinnamon, caster sugar and vinegar in a pot with 2 level teaspoons fine salt and 800ml water. Bring to the boil and simmer for 5 minutes. Drain the jar and pack with half the plums. Pour on half the liquid trying to make sure all the floating aromatics go in as well. Pack with the remaining plums and pour on the remaining simmering liquid. If the jar isn't full of liquid then top up with more hot liquid made by using 2 parts water to one part vinegar. Seal while hot and leave to cool, then place in the fridge and leave for at least 10 days, gently shaking the jar every few days.

Turn the oven to 180ºC. Cut the venison into two pieces to make it easier to fit into a pan if necessary. Mix the oregano with the olive oil, some salt and pepper and rub over the meat. Rest on a plate, cover with cling-film and bring to room temperature.

Bring a 2 litre pot of water to the boil then turn to a rapid simmer. Mix the flour and turmeric with 2 teaspoons fine salt and ¼ cup cold water until no lumps remain, then pour into the simmering water while whisking. Bring to the boil then add the salsify, rosemary and lemon and bring back to a rapid simmer. The salsify is cooked when you can just insert a thin knife into it – about 10 minutes. Drain into a colander and leave to cool on a tray, discarding the lemon.

Heat up a skillet or fry-pan and place the venison in and cook till browned all over. Transfer to a roasting dish and cook until somewhere between rare and medium rare– around 12-16 minutes depending on the thickness of the loin. Take from the oven and cover with foil and a tea-towel to keep the heat in and leave it to rest for 5 minutes.

Place another pan on the stove and add the butter and when it stops sizzling add the salsify with rosemary leaves attached and cook over moderate heat to warm through, tossing frequently.

Once it's hot sprinkle with the Parmigiano Reggiano and season.

Slice the plums, allowing ½ plum per person and divide on 6 warmed plates. Sit the salsify on, then cut the venison into 6 even sized chunks and tuck on top. Drizzle with the jus and sprinkle with the cress.

Wine suggestion: 2010 Waitaki Braids Pinot Noir, Waitaki Valley

A big thank you once again to Michael Seresin, Kevin Judd, Peter Gordon, Michael McGrath, Anna Hansen, Cristian Hossack and everyone else who generously contributed towards my 'Kiwi education' and enjoyment of your beautiful country.

To watch this roving sommelier video, please scan QR code with your smartphone

INDEX
&
WEB
LINKS

INDEX OF USEFUL REGIONAL INFORMATION, MAPS, LINKS TO WEBSITES, WINERIES, VINEYARDS, WINE REVIEWS AND VIDEOS.

Northland Vineyards and Wineries:

Greater Auckland Vineyards and Wineries

To get information, please scan QR code with your smartphone

Waikato Vineyards and Wineries:

Bay of Plenty Vineyards and Wineries

To get information, please scan QR code with your smartphone

AN EPICUREAN ODYSSEY

Gisborne Vineyards and Wineries

Hawke's Bay Vineyards and Wineries

To get information, please scan QR code with your smartphone

Wairarapa Vineyards and Wineries

Wines from Martinborough

To get information, please scan QR code with your smartphone

Wairarapa Maps and Directions

Wairarapa Visitor Information

To get information, please scan QR code with your smartphone

Marlborough Vineyards and Wineries

Marlborough Region

To get information, please scan QR code with your smartphone

Wine Marlborough

Marlborough Wine Trail Map

To get information, please scan QR code with your smartphone

Marlborough Wine and Food Festival

Tourism Links

To get information, please scan QR code with your smartphone

Marlborough Sub-regions

Sustainability

To get information, please scan QR code with your smartphone

Nelson Vineyards and Wineries:

Nelson as a region

To get information, please scan QR code with your smartphone

Nelson Wine Art

Otago Vineyards and Wineries:

To get information, please scan QR code with your smartphone

Central Otago Wine Map

Central Otago Regional Overview

To get information, please scan QR code with your smartphone

AN EPICUREAN ODYSSEY

Central Otago Pinot Noir

Waitaki Valley

To get information, please scan QR code with your smartphone

As we are all aware, this region and the city of Christchurch in particular suffered much damage during the earthquakes of 2009 and 2010. To my knowledge, most of the vineyards were not get affected. However, I strongly recommend seeking advice from the local tourist information to ascertain which are currently open. In addition, please make the necessary enquiries especially within Christchurch itself as some businesses may longer be there or may have moved locations.

Canterbury Vineyards and Wineries

To get information, please scan QR code with your smartphone

Canterbury Wine

Regional Vineyard Map

To get information, please scan QR code with your smartphone

Waipara Valley

Waipara Wine

AN EPICUREAN ODYSSEY

Waipara Valley Wine Trail

Waipara Valley Tours

To get information, please scan QR code with your smartphone

Waipara Valley Restaurants

Waipara Valley Accommodation

To get information, please scan QR code with your smartphone

Waipara Valley Wine and Food Festival

Summer of Riesling

To get information, please scan QR code with your smartphone

INTERESTING VIDEO BLOGS AND ARTICLES:

Video interviews

David Cox

A few words from Tina Gellie of Decanter Magazine

AN EPICUREAN ODYSSEY

Tim Heath of Cloudy Bay

Tim Heath on Cloudy Bay Pelorus

To get information, please scan QR code with your smartphone

Tim Heath on Riesling

Tim Heath on Sauvignon Blanc

Tim Heath on Late-harvest Riesling

Nick Lane on Cloudy Bay Te Koko

To get information, please scan QR code with your smartphone

Matt Thomson of Tinpot Hut talking about Gruner Veltliner

Tamra Washington introduces New Zealand Gruner Veltliner

Tamra Washington on Yealands Estate Gruner Veltliner

Tamra Washington on Seaview Vineyard and the Awatere Valley

To get information, please scan QR code with your smartphone

Tamra Washington on Yealands Estate Viognier

Richard Hendry on Coopers Creek Arneis

Richard Hendry on Coopers Creek Viognier

Mike Eaton (formerly of TerraVin) talking about Pinot Noir

To get information, please scan QR code with your smartphone

Katy Prescott of Nautilus summarises Marlborough Pinot Noir

Nick Lane of Cloudy Bay introduces Marlborough Pinot Noir

Nick Lane introduces Cloudy Bay Pinot Noir

Blair Walter of Felton Road speaking about "Calvert Vineyard"

To get information, please scan QR code with your smartphone

Nicola Greening of Felton Road

Steve Farquharson of The Wooing Tree Vineyard

Steve Farquharson telling "The Wooing Tree Blondie Story"

Dr John Forrest on Otago and Waitaki

To get information, please scan QR code with your smartphone

Sam Lockyer of Forrest Wines

Melanie Brown (nee Ellis) formerly of The Providores and currently owner of The New Zealand Cellar

Video montage of The Providores "Pop Up" with an interview with Tim Atkin MW speaking about New Zealand Syrah

Ronan Sayburn MS talking about his New Zealand experiences

To get information, please scan QR code with your smartphone

A very interactive and engaging video of Cloudy Bay Sauvignon Blanc being paired with food on the Chef's Table at The Montagu

Anna Hansen of The Modern Pantry

AN EPICUREAN ODYSSEY

Michael Seresin

Clive Dougall talking about Seresin wines

To get information, please scan QR code with your smartphone

Clive Dougall talking about biodynamics

Clive Dougall describes Seresin Chiaroscuro

AN EPICUREAN ODYSSEY

Clive Dougall explains Raupo Creek

Clive Dougall on "The Sun and The Moon"

To get information, please scan QR code with your smartphone

James Millton putting biodynamics in a nutshell

Larry McKenna of Escarpment Vineyard

AN EPICUREAN ODYSSEY

Lance Redgwell of Cambridge Road

Paul Mason of Martinborough Vineyards

To get information, please scan QR code with your smartphone

Steve Smith MW of Craggy Range on Martinborough Pinot Noir

Ant MacKenzie introduces Dry River and Martinborough

Ant MacKenzie on Dry River wines

Ant MacKenzie on Dry River's 'special' wine making ethos

To get information, please scan QR code with your smartphone

Richard Reed roasting coffee at Nude Espresso

Dr John Forrest remembers a wonderful hunting story

AN EPICUREAN ODYSSEY

A SELECTION OF USEFUL LINKS

New Zealand Winegrowers

New Zealand Family of Twelve

Pinot Noir New Zealand

Central Otago Pinot Noir

To get information, please scan QR code with your smartphone

The Specialist Winegrowers of New Zealand

New Zealand Wine Tours

To get information, please scan QR code with your smartphone

Of course, dear reader, I would like to end this epicurean odyssey on a positive note and leave you with an exquisite taste in your mouths. After all, I would like to think that I am good at my job.

The following menu would be my 'ultimate Kiwi meal experience'.

A plate of Bluff oysters
Quartz Reef "Methode Traditionelle", Central Otago

Laksa (The Providores)
Pegasus Bay, "Bel Canto", Riesling, Waipara

A big bowl of green-lipped mussels
Dog Point Vineyard "Section 94" Sauvignon Blanc, Marlborough

Classic Whitebait Fritter with two slices of bread and butter
Monteith's Golden Lager, Greymouth, West Coast

Perfect leg of Canterbury Lamb
Ata Rangi, Pinot Noir, Martinborough
Pegasus Bay "Prima Donna", Pinot Noir, Waipara

Roast venison with kumara gratin
Neudorf "Moutere" Pinot Noir, Nelson
Bilancia "La Collina" Syrah, Hawke's Bay

A selection of artisan cheeses from Whitestone Dairies
Pasquale, Pinot Gris, Waitaki Valley

Custard Tart
Craggy Range "Fletcher Vineyard", Late-harvest Riesling, Marlborough

ACKNOWLEDGEMENTS

I would like to thank the following: my parents, sister, family and friends for their love and support and all the kind people who generously helped with their time, advice and contributions towards this book. I would also like to acknowledge and thank all the people at New Zealand Wine Growers and The Family of Twelve (past and present).

You may be aware that I have always wanted to write a book. During 2009 (by this time I had become self-employed and was battling hard through serious depression) - I was actually trying to write two books at the same time. Of course, I quickly realised that this was a very silly thing to do. I summoned up all my strength, self-discipline and focus, and gathered all my thoughts, 'in-depth research' and material which have gone on to form this piece of work. Having travelled to New Zealand many times I certainly had plenty of anecdotes and experiences which have added a great deal of personality and life to this journey.

Subsequently, now, and more than four years later since its initial publication, I have realised that I have accumulated more material and fresh content and even more evocative memories with which I am able to produce a revised edition of the original.

To be honest with such an emotional attachment to New Zealand it has been quite a cathartic process, especially having seriously considered the possibility of living there. But, this time I have found my 'return journey' has been profoundly positive and personally rewarding on many levels. Having authored my second book "Sommelier Stories" and my third "A Bucket List of New Zealand Wines", I have also realised what the most important things in life are, those things we hold so dear and everything else really does not matter. After all, for me the greatest prize is an intense love I discovered years ago.

One of my biggest of inspirations to put pen to paper were the courageous people of New Zealand. During 2009 and 2010, the city of Christchurch was hit by two terrible earthquakes which caused much devastation. I visited many of those places only months beforehand, most of which were completely destroyed, including its gothic cathedral and mighty stadium. That rugby-mad city lost more than 180 people and more recently the nation's capital, Wellington suffered more damage during more earthquakes. Returning to both cities during spending a few months in New Zealand in 2014 was incredibly uplifting. In fact, my time in Christchurch on this occasion was really inspiring and was a pure demonstration of the city's spirit and positive energy. For me, the people of this beautiful country are the real heroes. I wish you safe travels around New Zealand and I am really looking forward to hearing about your own stories.

Most importantly I would like to dedicate this book to my late mother who sadly passed away far too soon in January 2014 after suffering from cancer.

In the meantime, even though she now resides in Brisbane, I believe that it is my ultimate destiny to be re-united once again with the love of my life, my soul-mate forever, Sandy.

Arohanui.

You can also connect with me at the following websites:

www.rovingsommelier.com
www.anepicureanodyssey.com

Follow our tweets and updates on Twitter @rovingsommelier.
and connect with us at our Official Facebook page
www.facebook.com/rovingsommelier

The epicurean odyssey continues...

Lightning Source UK Ltd.
Milton Keynes UK
UKHW010704261119
354262UK00001B/21/P

9 781291 521696